MARK HUNTER | "THE SALES HUNTER"

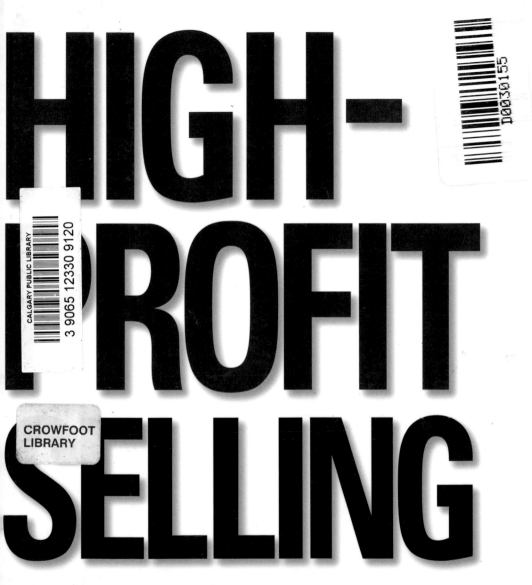

HIGH-PROFIT SELLING

WIN THE SALE WITHOUT COMPROMISING ON PRICE

Advance Praise for *High-Profit Selling*

"If you are in sales, you simply can't let your motivation—or your profits—slide. You owe it to yourself and your career to grab a copy of *High-Profit Selling*. Mark Hunter gives you the leverage you need to succeed."—**Chris Widener, author of** *The Art of Influence* **and** *Leadership Rules*

"After reading Mark Hunter's new book I would absolutely not only add it to my sales library, I would recommend adding it to your sales training curriculum. I would recommend that each of your salespeople read this book and then schedule a weekly sales meeting to discuss each chapter and how it relates to your sales process. Your sales will explode!"—**Ken Thoreson, Acumen Management Group, and author of** *Your Sales Management: Guru's Guide to Leading High Performance Sales Teams*

"There are some key fundamentals in B2B selling, without which you will not have consistent success. Understanding and teaching those fundamentals takes special knowledge and skill. Mark Hunter has not only that knowledge and skill but a unique ability to get others to adopt and use them in improving and increasing their sales. Now you can take advantage of that for you and your team with Mark's book, *High-Profit Selling*. If you are looking to increase both the top and bottom lines, Mark's book is a must."—**Tibor Shanto, Renbor Sales Solutions, and coauthor of** *SHIFT: Harness the Trigger Events that Turn Prospects into Customers*

"High-profit selling in this environment is a considerable challenge, but Mark Hunter gives you all the tools you'll need in this one book to succeed . . . profitably!"—**Joe Bourland, Director, Category Management, North America, Kimberly-Clark Corporation**

"Finally a book on sales that tells it like it is. It's not the economy or territory or customer that's holding you back. Rather, it's up to you. Mark gives you the specific tools to get better, make more money, and feel great about being in sales. A true classic and must-read for any sales professional or business owner."—**Mike Brooks, "Mr. Inside Sales," author of** *The Real Secrets of the Top 20%: How to Double Your Income Selling Over the Phone*

"In a tight economy, salespeople need as many tools as possible to make the most profit on each sale. If your selling strategy seems stale and ineffective, revolutionize it today with *High-Profit Selling*. Mark Hunter delivers the goods on this one!"—**Wendy Weiss, the "Queen of Cold Calling™," and author of** *Cold Calling for Women: Opening Doors and Closing Sales* **and** *The Sales Winner's Handbook: Essential Scripts & Strategies to Skyrocket Sales Performance*

"Mark Hunter brings wit and wisdom to the serious business of big time sales. It's not just philosophy. Mark delivers the inspiration you need to be a superstar."—**Dan Waldschmidt, EdgyConversations.com**

"*High-Profit Selling* drives home a vital message regarding price. It's almost impossible to win on price alone, and Mark Hunter makes that clear and easy to understand."—**Kenny Herbst, Marketing Professor, Schools of Business, Wake Forest University**

"This book shows that clients *will* pay for value. Mark has done it, and now you get to see his successful methods.—**Tom Greco, Senior Vice President of Business Development, Ipsos ASI**

"A writer's job is to tell the truth, and Mark Hunter does exactly that. Forget what you learned. Focus on the bottom line, tell the ROI story, and never fight the price war."—**Joanne S. Black, founder, No More Cold Calling®, and author of** *No More Cold Calling™: The Breakthrough System That Will Leave Your Competition in the Dust*

"If you want to produce more business at the zenith of profit margins (don't we all!), *High-Profit Selling* is your ticket to Valhalla. Mark Hunter's expertise on this vital point of selling is unequaled. You're probably going to send him a thank-you letter for all the extra income he puts into your pocket."—**Robert Terson, SellingFearlessly.com**

"In a time of shrinking margins, Mark gives practical insights and advice on how to increase profit margins. Very inspiring!"—**Steven Rosen, founder and President, STAR Results, a sales leadership, training, and consulting organization**

"Mark's profound and grounded insights are not just for the largest corporate client, but are equally important for the many small businesses who mistakenly think they need to compete on price. In this book, Mark demonstrates why superior selling is not about making the sale but growing the bottom line for both you and your customers."—**Dr. Dale T. Eesley, Director, Center** for Innovation, Entrepreneurship, and Franchising, University of Nebraska at Omaha

"Mark Hunter hits the mark in *High-Profit Selling*! It's filled with personal stories and Mark's proven methods to sell more effectively and successfully. This is a great resource for salespeople!—**Kelly McCormick, author of *Out-Sell Yourself: Go from Hello to Sold with Ethical Business and Sales Techniques!***

"The sales space is pregnant with over-hyped rhetoric and vanilla, myopic, self-serving banality right now. Fortunately, we have a handful of forward thinking commentators who have served their time in the trenches and are able to draw on that experience to educate others. Mark is one of those few, as this book amply illustrates."—**Jonathan Farrington, chairman, The JF Corporation, and CEO, Top Sales Associates and Top Sales World**

A must-read for every company and salesperson looking to grow their businesses and maximize their profits.—**Angelo Gioia, Executive Director of Agents of America.org**

Sales professionals who understand and implement the new paradigms of selling have the advantage. Read *High-Profit Selling* before your competition does.—**Mace Horoff, Sales Pilot at Mastering Medical Sales**

An innovative and practical set of ideas for framing the price discussion in a way that optimizes sales profitability. An important book about an important topic.—**Richard Ruff, Ph.D., Managing Partner of Sales Horizons and co-author of *Managing Major Sales***

"Mark Hunter's ability to make a complex sales challenge become a simplified, crystalized step-by-step solution is unmatched. He can truly increase your organization's profitability with strong, repeatable sales processes that carry his integrity and excitement for business."—**Gus Gustafson, FullyArmed.com**

"*High-Profit Selling* is a book well positioned for today's economy, packed with road-tested tips and strategies."—**Michael Geiger, JET Equipment & Tools Ltd.**

"Mark Hunter is truly an expert at motivation and sales and someone I would demand being next to in the trenches."—**Dan Borschke, Executive Director, National Association of Concessionaires**

"Lowering prices leads to increasing sales . . . but also to decreasing profit. Finally, a book that teaches rather brilliantly the way out of this marketing madness."—**Frank Gamez, founder, Ideas Nuevas**

"In today's competitive marketplace, price is becoming more prevalent in discussions with customers. This book provides practical insights to help you avoid discussions based solely on price and to deliver highly profitable solutions to customers, creating long-term value and loyalty."—**Steve Gavatorta, President, Steve Gavatorta Group, and author of** *The Reach Out Approach: A Communication Process for Initiating, Developing, and Leveraging Mutually Rewarding Relationships*

"Mark Hunter is an astute sales coach who lives what he talks. His material and methodology are driven by his personal successes within the sales field."—**Bart McCoy, Vice President, Business Development, Lee Hecht Harrison**

"Mark Hunter taught me sales methods that helped me exponentially grow my preemployment testing business. And now, in his book sales reps and executives can learn Mark's sales expertise and put it into action to dramatically grow their businesses." --**Michael Mercer, Ph.D., author of** *Hire the Best . . . & Avoid the Rest*

"Mark has a unique ability to break down complex subject areas into simple and actionable steps that generate immediate results."—**Jon Halpern, Vice President, Kantar Retail**

HIGH-PROFIT SELLING

Win the Sale Without Compromising on Price

Mark Hunter

American Management Association

New York • Atlanta • Brussels • Chicago • Mexico City • San Francisco
Shanghai • Tokyo • Toronto • Washington, D.C.

This publication is designed to provide accurate and authoritative information in regard to the subject matter covered. It is sold with the understanding that the publisher is not engaged in rendering legal, accounting, or other professional service. If legal advice or other expert assistance is required, the services of a competent professional person should be sought.

Library of Congress Cataloging-in-Publication Data

Hunter, Mark, 1956–
    High-profit selling : win the sale without compromising on price / Mark Hunter.
        p.   cm.
    Includes index.
    ISBN-13: 978-0-8144-2009-6
    ISBN-10: 0-8144-2009-5
1. Selling.   I. Title.
    HF5438.25.H8674   2012
    658.85—dc23

                                                                        2011041503

About AMA

American Management Association (www.amanet.org) is a world leader in talent development, advancing the skills of individuals to drive business success. Our mission is to support the goals of individuals and organizations through a complete range of products and services, including classroom and virtual seminars, webcasts, webinars, podcasts, conferences, corporate and government solutions, business books, and research. AMA's approach to improving performance combines experiential learning—learning through doing—with opportunities for ongoing professional growth at every step of one's career journey.

Printing number
10   9   8   7   6   5   4   3   2   1

Contents

Introduction

OVER THE YEARS, I've been amazed at the number of times salespeople have asked me how they can avoid lowering a price to close a deal. As many times as I've been asked, I know there are hundreds more salespeople wondering the same thing. The tactic of giving someone a lower price as an incentive to close a deal is certainly not new. It has been going on for as long as there have been people looking to sell something to someone else. What astounds me, though, is that cutting prices to close a deal seems to happen regardless of whether the item is staggeringly expensive or supercheap. Customers want a deal, and too many salespeople are more than willing to give that deal, regardless of the negative consequences.

But will the customer buy if the price *isn't* lowered? This is a vital piece of information to have if you want to close the deal. Unfortunately, many salespeople don't dig deep enough to find the answer. The end result is the salesperson simply resorts to lowering the price. When the salesperson gives in once on price, the sales process usually becomes a game where customers wait to see how low they can get the salesperson to go on price—*and everything else.* Profits continue to erode at an expanding rate until the damage is done (and even then, some salespeople still don't realize the extent of the damage).

The purpose of this book is to show you how you can avoid cutting prices to close sales. I'll even show you that instead of cutting prices, in many cases you actually can raise them! For some of you, this is an unheard-of concept because never has a week gone by in your selling career that didn't involve lowering price, regardless of the impact on you or your company.

I am dedicated to showing salespeople how to avoid this habit of discounting. While it is definitely possible to stay firm on your price (and even raise it), I'm not saying it is easy. If you are looking for a couple of quick, easy steps, this book isn't for you. If, however, you want to make solid changes in your sales process that will lead to high-profit selling, then you have arrived at the right place. I will walk you through each phase of the selling process, from finding the right prospects to closing the sale. You will learn the techniques and ideas that you can best adapt for your situation and industry.

The core of the problem rarely is a customer who is not willing to pay. Rather, I believe the problem begins with salespeople who do not believe in the price they are asking. If the salesperson does not believe in the price, then there is no way the customer will ever choose to pay anything that is not discounted. Harboring internal doubts about price affects the salesperson's ability to close sales and, more important, to ensure the profit margin.

In this book I'll share personal stories—good and bad—about how I have dealt with issues on sales calls. The experiences cover a cross section of my more than twenty-five years as a salesperson and now as a consultant and speaker on sales and, particularly, on pricing. I think you will find that my stories are similar to situations you have already faced or are currently facing.

Many salespeople claim that price is one of the biggest issues they confront when closing a sale. To me, it's debatable whether price is genuinely a big issue or simply something we have come to believe is a big issue. I devote considerable time in this book to helping you determine whether price is the real, underlying issue holding back a sale or if the customer is merely *saying* it is the issue. More important, I'll show you how to respond to the customer and even how to avoid getting into situations where price becomes the central focus. It may surprise you, but when selling situations are consumed with discussion about price, it usually means the salesperson is dealing with the wrong type of customer. You want customers who are focused less on price and more on how your product or service meets their needs and delivers desired benefits.

High-profit selling is all about changing how you think. If you change how you think, you can then change how you deal with the customer. By changing how you deal with the customer, you can take control of the process and move yourself away from dependence on discounting to closing sales.

In all my years in the selling profession, I have seen countless techniques that customers use to try to get a salesperson to lower the price. I will walk you through the more prevalent situations, including how to handle professional buyers and requests for proposals. My goal is to offer you solid solutions for the problems you face. After reading this book, you'll be better prepared to go into your next sales call without relying on discounting to actually close the sale. Finally, I'll share with you the exact steps you need to take to avoid the many problems that can arise when a company attempts to increase its price.

High-profit selling sounds good, doesn't it? It does to me! Let me show you that there is nothing wrong with high profits when they allow both you and the customer to win.

You Are Hurting Your Profit

SOME PEOPLE PLACE THE BLAME for anything that goes wrong on someone or something else. This has become the norm today with far too many salespeople. They blame their inability to make the sale on everything except the fact that they are unable to present a compelling reason for customers to buy from them.

If you were to ask salespeople why they can't close more sales, many of them would claim it is because their price is too high and simply more than what their customers want to spend. I've heard this excuse thousands of times. I can't begin to tell you how often I've seen marketing departments and sales executives get sucked into believing it. But in reality, price is only one of many factors that influence people or companies to buy. Even if you are in a business where you sell commodities, there are other issues, such as quantity, delivery time, shipping method, and payment terms, that influence the customer's buying decision. Unfortunately, many salespeople have the tendency to turn this one element—price—into the *only* issue.

The business environment is tough. There are always outside factors beyond the control of the salesperson that can and will affect how customers behave. Whether the economy is up or down, it seems that customers are asking for a discount or saying they won't pay the listed price. It's time we slay the myth that selling revolves around price. I can dispel this false concept for you, both in your personal sales process and in your entire company, so that you can stop hurting your profit and actually start increasing it.

In this book, I'll show you how to get the customer to accept your price. Beyond that, I'm also going to show you how to increase your price *and* have your customer thank you for charging more. Yes, you read that right! I'm going to help you to convince your customer that there's a higher level of value reflected in the higher prices you are charging, which is representative of both you and what you are selling. You may be wondering if I've lost my mind. It's okay to doubt me, because it means that once I show you and, more important, *convince* you that you can turn a higher price in your favor, you'll embrace my recommendations even more.

Ask yourself:

Would I be a better salesperson if I could generate 20 percent more profit off the same amount of sales?

Now ask yourself:

If I could increase the value of what I'm selling in the eyes of my customer, how much more profit would that be worth to me?

Finally, ask yourself:

If all it took was 30 minutes a day to increase my overall sales performance by 30 percent, would it be worth it?

I bet I know how you'd answer each of these questions. The questions themselves are not tough to answer. The challenge is in figuring out how to proceed after you have answered them. You obviously care enough about improving your profitability to have bought this book, so I have no doubt that you *want* to do what it takes. I'm committed to helping you.

What Is This Book Worth to You?

Reread the previous paragraph and you'll notice that I didn't mention the price of this book. I pointed out the value of what you are going to get from it. I set up a scenario and got you to do some self-reflecting. By merely going through this exercise, you've begun to determine what the price/value relationship is for *High-Profit Selling*. Some of you may see the book as a tool for potentially unlocking $1 million in increased profitability for your company each year. Others may see a $50,000 annual opportunity, while still others may see only $1,000 per year. What would the value of this book be if the increase in profitability you gain from it occurs each year for the next ten years?

Regardless of the specific increase in profitability you may potentially realize, you have an expected benefit for the book—and this expected benefit plays immediately into the price you are willing to pay for it.

What if the price of the book could vary by an amount reflecting the full value of what somebody would gain from it? If that were possible, then some people would pay $20 while others would pay $20,000. Naturally, this is not possible. I use this example because I recognize that in some situations it's not possible to vary the price or some other part of the price equation. These circumstances can make your role as a salesperson more difficult. However, the premise of this book is that you must find a way to increase profit whatever the situation.

To increase your profit you may have to find other ways to enable the customer to receive value, which means you need to have different strategies and tactics to help you through all situations. Throughout this book I'll show you how to do just that.

To Maximize Profit, Change How You View Your Customers

You must be able to provide your customers with the services and/or products they want in a manner that allows you to maximize your profit. To that end, you have to change the way you view your customers. The solution lies in seeing each customer as having unique needs that require a unique solution from you. When you view your customers in this way, you will discover new opportunities to assist them and they in turn will be willing to pay more for these solutions.

Maximizing your profit also requires that you assess your service or product offerings to tailor them more effectively to what the customer wants. Don't worry, I'm not proposing changes to your manufacturing or supply-chain systems. In the vast majority of selling situations, maximizing profit does not require any changes to your internal process. The changes you'll need to make are to your selling process and how you deal with your customer. This is why I say high-profit selling is all about *you*. When you, the salesperson, take ownership of the complete selling process and the customer, it's amazing what can and will happen.

It's Time to Look in the Mirror

Throughout this book you'll find countless proven methods for selling more effectively and successfully. But before you can begin to put even the first principle to work, you have to look in the mirror and assess yourself. Don't look for others to be your key to success. More than anything else, it's sales motivation that counts. The less sales motivation you have, the more profit is lost. Sales motivation is composed of your attitude and your confidence. You can have the greatest product in your industry or niche, you can have unbelievable advertising or fabulous marketing materials, but you can still lose sales if your attitude is poor and you lack confidence.

In my years as a sales consultant to corporations large and small around the globe, I've sat across the desk from many marketing and/or sales VPs and told them not to spend one more penny on advertising or marketing until they fix the problems with their sales force. I look them in the eye and say they must look closely at their team's level of confidence in what they are doing and what they are selling. Yes, this critique has made for some tense situations, but I'm a firm believer in making sure that sales can handle what marketing will deliver.

The example I like to use is that there's no sense in owning a Lamborghini if you don't know how to drive it. You'll never be able to fully appreciate its qualities unless you are skilled at driving a high-performance car. The same applies in sales. We all have the ability to communicate with customers, but do we all have the ability to truly sell? If you don't possess the best selling skills, there's no way you'll ever be able to fully use the opportunities that marketing may give to you.

If you think I'm putting marketing on a pedestal, I assure you that's not the case. I've been in sales for more than twenty-five years, and during that time I've grown skeptical of what the typical marketing department claims it can do. I believe that sales and marketing must work together cohesively if either is going to achieve its goals. Think of it this way: Sales and marketing are connected in a food chain. Marketing creates the food that sales eats. There's no reason for marketing to create anything that sales can't eat. At the same time, there's no reason for sales to ask marketing to make anything that sales won't eat.

Your Confidence Drives Your Attitude

Your level of confidence drives how much you believe in what you sell and how you deal with your customers. Unfortunately, too many salespeople lack complete confidence in what they sell and, therefore, in the price they are expected to charge. Why? The simple fact is that the vast majority of salespeople are not willing to take personal responsibility for failing to close more sales.

If we were to believe that the reason salespeople are not more successful is simply because of pricing, then all we'd have to do to solve the problem is lower the price we ask for our goods or services. The problem with this line of thinking is that no matter how much you lower your price, you are almost always cutting your profits by a percentage far greater than the percentage of the price reduction. Salespeople often fail to realize the damage they are doing to themselves, and to their business, by thinking they can close more sales by taking this price-cutting approach.

The other problem with lowering the price to close more sales is that there's no guarantee the competition won't do the same thing. And what's to say the customer isn't going to continue to demand further price reductions? Either way, you lose. What's the point of selling anything if you are unable to make any money from the sale? This is why you must establish, in the mind of your customers, the value they will receive at the price you offer.

The level of confidence you must have is not just in the product or service you are selling, but also in the price you are asking. Let's dig into this idea by using a comparison of two companies and the different ways in which they determine the price they ask for the same item.

Can a Company Asking a Higher Price Really Win?

Here's an example I frequently use when addressing sales organizations: One company, which we'll call Ace, is struggling to grow, but the products it makes are very good. Ace is a smaller player in the marketplace and establishes its pricing based on what it costs to make the product. The company's managers have done repeated analysis of their cost structure and know exactly what it costs to make their goods; therefore, they know exactly how to price them based on these costs.

A second company, which we'll call Big, is a large, well-financed, multinational organization that produces the same item as Ace. But Big does not price its product based on what it costs to produce. Instead, Big bases the product's price on the value its customers see in the product. The entire sales process is all about helping customers realize the value of what they are buying. More important, Big has excelled at showing customers how the product helps them deal with their critical needs.

By now you probably know where I'm going with this story. The company that is able to get a much higher price is Big. The real issue, though, is that the salespeople who work for Ace are nothing more than order takers who fail to maximize their relationships with their customers. In fact, I would go as far as to say that Big's customers probably appreciate the relationship they have with Big more than Ace's customers appreciate Ace. Big clearly is focused on helping its customers see how they are getting a superior value.

Are you beginning to grasp this vital concept? Value is what the customer believes it is, not what the salesperson thinks it is. In too many selling situations, you may be doing way too much thinking! That is, when you focus too much about how you define value, and you try to sell that idea of value to someone else, it can start knocking down your confidence. As your confidence gets knocked down, your attitude starts to suffer, and suddenly you are in a vicious downward spiral. A better approach is to allow your customers to define value for you.

Confidence—in yourself and in what you sell—is without a doubt the greatest single asset you can bring to both your customers and your profitability. Your challenge is my challenge, because I'm committed to helping you find ways to increase your level of confidence in the prices you offer. Note the last word in the previous sentence is "offer" not "charge." Confident salespeople don't *charge* anybody anything, so strike that word from your vocabulary from this point on. Rather, confident salespeople allow their customers to invest in, to participate in, and to benefit from their offerings. It doesn't matter whether you sell in a business-to-business environment or a business-to-consumer environment. The principle is the same.

People Don't Buy—They Only Invest

Customers don't want to buy. They only want to invest in order to achieve something: to get some sort of gain or to relieve a pain. For example, a company may be looking to buy insurance to minimize the risk of theft or vandalism; this would be an investment to relieve a pain. The company is only going to invest enough money in buying insurance to offset what it sees as the risk. If the company believes the potential loss from theft (i.e., the pain the company would suffer) would not be very much, it might make the decision not to buy insurance. An example of a gain that a company might invest in would be buying a new piece of equipment to help operations run more efficiently. In both these cases, the company will invest if it can get a clear return on investment. Although the cost (price) is factored into the decision, it is really the return on that cost that is most important—so price is a secondary consideration.

While these examples involve businesses, the concept applies equally to individual customers. They are also looking to gain something or to relieve pain when they are contemplating making a purchase—or, should I say, looking to invest.

Confident salespeople help their customers succeed, and that's exactly what you are doing when you sell something. For instance, I have a high degree of confidence in what I do as a consultative sales expert because I firmly believe I'm helping you and thousands of others achieve a higher level of profit from each sale.

An exercise I like to take salespeople through to help them develop their confidence is to ask them to write the top-five reasons customers buy from them. I then ask them to detail specifically what benefits their customers gain from the purchase. Do this exercise for yourself and keep your written answers someplace where you can refer to them regularly. Also, ask some of your loyal customers what benefits they are getting from buying from you. They might mention some things you haven't thought of. The idea is to always have in the front of your mind the reasons customers prefer to do business with you rather than your competitors. If salespeople have no idea why their customers do business with them, it's no wonder so many of them struggle with the issue of maximizing price!

Forget About Your Competition

Too much effort is lost worrying about what a competitor is charging. Forget about your competition. They are not you. It's time for you to be proud of who you are. People who second-guess themselves are never going to excel. Would you choose to follow someone who wasn't sure of himself? How, then, can we expect customers to pay a premium price for anything if the salespeople they are dealing with are always second-guessing themselves?

Even if you sell commodity items, and no matter how price-sensitive the market is in which you compete, there are still reasons, besides price, that sway customers. So, as you develop your list of reasons why your customers buy from you, don't include price as one of them. Take your time to expand your list, and be sure to get input from your customers. When you ask them why they buy from you, you'll be pleasantly surprised at what you hear. More often than not, they will tell you positive news.

This book is designed to give you the tools you need to succeed. Confident people accept ownership of their situation, and they readily accept responsibility for who they are, as well as for their actions. More important, they are comfortable knowing they will be judged not only on what happens to them, but on how they choose to respond to what happens to them.

Start with this premise: More than anything else, you and you alone are the reason you are able to command the prices you are asking from your customers. When you position yourself as the confident source assisting them, then the profit you make will be commensurate with the benefits the customers are receiving. Do this and both you and your customer win.

"Profit" Is Not a Dirty Word

ROFIT. What does that word mean to you? Too often, profit is seen as something dirty, something only greedy people are looking to gain. Many people think profit means that someone is taking advantage of someone else by charging too much. These perceptions bother me, as they should anyone else who understands business. Profit is an absolutely essential outcome of capitalism, and it is far from being a dirty word. In my view, profit is something similar to oil in an engine. For an engine to run effectively, it requires oil. For a business to operate effectively, it requires profit.

Profit can also be viewed as a scorecard of a company's success and as the foundation of research and development. When a business provides its customers with what they need

17

and want, it is able to make a profit. The company can then use this profit to do any number of things, but one of them is to reinvest in the business in order to be able to serve customers even better.

The objective of this chapter is to show you the value of profit and what it can do for your business. In particular, this chapter emphasizes why you need to strive to maximize the profit you make on every sale.

Are You Chasing the Shiny Object?

It's easy to become distracted by the latest trend, an idea that seems too good to ignore. This habit is commonly referred to as "chasing the shiny object." Your salespeople start trying to break into new areas that are suddenly "hot" or go after prospects whose businesses look as if they will give your company's reputation a real boost. Companies and salespeople lose sight of the fact that the real objective of every company is not to chase the latest fad, but to make a profit. If a company isn't making a profit, it doesn't matter how well its salespeople have perfected the latest trendy technique or how many big-name clients they acquire.

Salespeople tend to forget the importance of profit because it is more exciting to chase the shiny object. Somewhere along the way, the salesperson becomes distracted and sales suffer. My own sales career has been adversely affected by this problem. I've experienced major bouts of this "getting distracted disease," both while working for major corporations and when self-employed. You might say this disease doesn't show favoritism—it strikes everybody. And each time it strikes, it comes at the expense of profit.

An example I like to share comes from my own experiences in the first few months after launching a new consulting business. Before the launch I developed a business plan that included a very tight price list from which I would work when talking to clients. I developed the price list to ensure I made a nice level of profit that I would be able to reinvest into the business and ultimately make it grow.

My problem began early on when I had a prospect with lots of potential who wasn't going to accept my pricing arrangement. I believed this prospect represented such a huge long-term opportunity that it was worth lowering my price. Fatal mistake! I fell for the shiny object, believing the long-term potential would offset what I thought would be the short-term loss of profit.

Several things happened as a result of my mistake. First, I got the project, and it did create cash flow, but it didn't leave me with enough profit to build my business. Second, because I had lowered my price, this client now had a value expectation at a lower price. This created a significant issue for me when I tried to convince the client to accept a higher price when it came time to renew the contract. Third, a problem occurred that was clearly the most damaging in destroying my pricing confidence. After reducing my price for one customer, I allowed myself to believe it would be okay, maybe even necessary, to close the next deal at a lower price point as well—to get a few early sales in the bag to build up some cash. I was revising my prices downward only because I thought the profit I had originally factored into the sale was more than adequate. The overall results, as you might expect, were negative both in the short term and in the long term.

When speaking to sales groups, I like to share this example because everybody can relate to it in one way or another. It's easy now to look back and see the obvious mistakes I made. The lessons I've learned along the way are numerous. Each time I think I have a complete list of everything that can be learned in regard to profit, somebody comes up to me and shares still one more lesson worth learning.

Do *You* Think "Profit" Is a Dirty Word?

Let's examine the *hows* and the *whys* that drive salespeople to believe that profit is something they don't need to be concerned about. In general, salespeople are motivated by a twofold objective: pleasing the customer and making money. That phrase right there sums it all up: *Pleasing the customer* comes first and *making money* comes second. Too many salespeople become distracted by thinking too much about why the customer won't do business with them and subsequently conclude that the reason, plain and simple, is price. Yes, the disease of chasing the sale no matter the consequence shows up in many different ways, but the ultimate outcome that hurts the most is a loss of profit.

I'm very passionate about this problem for a number of reasons, but the strongest one is because I've felt the pain personally. I want to help as many people as possible to avoid such pain.

The best way to deal with a problem is to face it head-on. I believe dealing with profit is one of the top-two issues salespeople have. (The other is prospecting, which I'll discuss in Chapter 5.)

How Do We Define "Profit?"

There are several ways that I advise senior management and salespeople to look at profit. First, they need to look at the *immediate profit* they are earning monthly, quarterly, and annually. Second, they need to look at what I refer to as the *profit sustainability factor,* or PSF. This measurement is all about understanding the profit potential the customer may provide you over a long period of time (e.g., several years). PSF is a critical measure for sales managers to use with regard to how much attention they are going to focus on a specific customer. Finally, senior management and salespeople need to look at *intellectual profitability,* of which there are two types. The first is found in your ability to make the customer feel comfortable buying from you and recommending you to others. The other type of intellectual profitability involves situations where you are able to learn a key lesson that can then be used with other customers.

No one who calls himself a salesperson can overlook these three measurements of profit. From that angle, every employee in the company is a salesperson.

What Does "Immediate Profit" Mean?

A few years back I was working with a salesperson who felt guilty about the profit margins her company was making. She sincerely felt that it wasn't right for the company to charge the prices it was charging. I found it amazing how quickly she would offer a prospect a discount or be willing to add on an additional service at no extra charge. I was *not* surprised at how quickly each prospect took advantage of these offers.

Sure, this salesperson was successful in closing sales, but then again, who wouldn't be successful in sales by lowering the price enough? In reality, she was actually eroding her company's profit base. The company was not making the profit it expected on each sale. To compound the matter, the customers were walking away with a mistaken view of the cost-value benefit of what they had bought.

As you can imagine, it made for some very unhappy customers when, a year or so later, they were faced with the new price the company would be charging them. They were unhappy because they had come to believe they would pay a certain amount for the service. They built their business model around it, only to find out later that the new price would be considerably higher or they would have to go without certain services they had come to expect. Either way, the result is not positive; customers rarely understand or even care how they wound up with a lower first-year price. Consequently, the sales force had to spend too much time in year two reselling the entire value proposition.

This example shows not only how dollar profit can be eroded immediately, but also how there is a negative impact on the salesperson's time. Salespeople often overlook the fact that their own time is one of the most critical assets they need to manage. *Time* and *profit* are interdependent. The salesperson who was quick to discount her profit bought herself some time up-front by closing the sale faster. However, she was going to lose time when she had to come back to customers at a later date and sell them on the higher, nondiscounted price. Keep in mind that even when salespeople are successful in selling the customer the nondiscounted price, they have still lost money because it doesn't make up for the profit given up with the initial sale.

As a salesperson, you have to fully commit to maximizing profit. That means you must expect the customer to pay full price right from the start. The sooner you realize this fact, the better off you are. I often run into salespeople who say they understand the importance of profit, but then they turn around and contradict themselves by offering a discount or throwing in something "extra" for free. Each time you make even the slightest change to an order, you run the risk of costing your company money. Every time you are not successful in closing a sale and need to make a follow-up sales call to the customer, you are costing your company profit.

Profit made by you and your company is what fuels the next round of product improvements. It allows your company to spend more money on marketing. It provides investors with reasons they should invest even more money in the company. A very simple equation I use is that all salespeople need to find a way to increase the level of profit they contribute to their employer by at least 10 percent each year to ensure the company will have the funds necessary to grow. The 10 percent number is a minimum—a common growth number in sales. There are many industries where 10 percent is just a start.

There's no such thing as a onetime discount. Although most of us have tried, at one time or another, to convince ourselves that we are giving a "onetime discount" to a particular customer, the simple fact is that nobody has enough resolve or sales motivation to stick to the offer of a "onetime" discount. As soon as you do it once, you'll do it again the next time. That's human nature. Once you get into the habit of offering a price reduction, it becomes almost routine.

In later chapters, I'll show you specific steps you can take to minimize this problem, but for now, let me offer one idea in which I believe strongly: Sales managers should not give *any* pricing latitude to salespeople. If your salespeople can't offer a discount, they won't. It's that simple. Now, I know salespeople will come up with all kinds of reasons that they need to be able to offer a discount. I've found, though, after working with thousands of salespeople in numerous industries, that the vast majority of the time, the salesperson who does not have the latitude to discount will bring in more profit than the salesperson who is allowed to discount.

What Is Your Customer Worth Down the Road?

The second type of profit, as mentioned previously, is profit sustainability factor (PSF). This is a key indicator that every sales manager or salesperson needs to use to understand how much time a salesperson should devote to a new customer. Remember, a key piece of profit is the salesperson's time, so PSF is a critical tool in determining how to use resources. PSF is all about knowing *how much profit a customer is worth over a long period of time.* It might be three years or ten years, or any other time period of your choosing, but it provides you with a gauge to evaluate the right amount of time to spend closing the initial sale.

Sales managers can sometimes be too shortsighted in terms of allocating resources. They fall behind in their numbers, so they start chasing the quick sale (again, the "shiny object"). They allow attention to be diverted away from the large-opportunity prospect that could, in the long term, provide a steady stream of profit.

As you lay out your annual goals, it's important to allocate your time accurately. You need to ensure you have the proper amount of time to spend on customers from whom you will realize a profit right away, as well as larger-profit customers who will take longer to close but will ultimately pay off much more down the road.

A very simple rule is to spend more of your time at the start of your sales period with longer-term customers who have a high PSF. Then, as the sales period moves along, you should increase your selling time with the customers that will result in an immediate profit. This is especially true when it comes to using CEOs and other senior-level executives on sales calls. I strongly recommend that senior-level people make more sales calls at the beginning of the fiscal year to help lay the groundwork with high PSF customers. This runs counter to how most senior executives use their time. Many believe they should go out at the end of the fiscal period to help close as many sales as possible. This strategy can be beneficial, it's true, but if it becomes the norm, then the entire sales process begins to be slanted toward this method: Lower-level salespeople bring the customer to a certain point, after which senior company officials then come in and close the sale.

There are some real risks with this approach. For one, the salesperson loses confidence and credibility with the customer because too often when the CEO or other senior executives are brought in at the eleventh hour, they will more likely make a concession to get the deal. When this happens, several new issues suddenly emerge. Not only has the CEO's or senior manager's time been used ineffectively, but it ends up resulting in a loss of profit. So, it's a double loss. If you work in an industry where buyers move between companies, then there's an added negative impact, because soon the message spreads and people learn not to buy from your company until they get a sales call from a senior officer (who will inevitably offer a concession).

Sounds like a crazy scenario, doesn't it? I tell you from experience that it happens more often than salespeople realize. Smart buyers watch for these types of behaviors, and when they spot them with a vendor, they'll routinely delay a purchase until they get a visit from a senior-level person late in the vendor's fiscal year.

Calculate Your Customer's Profitability Sustainability Factor

Let's get back to the formula for determining the PSF. It's a combination of the probability of the customer continuing to do business with you, compared to the anticipated profit you expect to earn from the customer, less the cost of selling and servicing the customer. The exact formula will vary by industry. Economic factors and competitive issues also affect it. However, there are two key rules I always use when developing the PSF:

Rule 1. The cost to acquire the customer will always be more than expected.

Rule 2. The profitability of the customer will generally peak about the third year of the relationship and then go into a slow descent.

Let me explain that last point: Often a customer relationship becomes unprofitable after a number of years, even though it is rarely recognized as such by salespeople. As time passes, salespeople erroneously assume that because a customer has been around for a long time, that customer must still be profitable. What actually happens is that the longer a customer sticks around, the tighter the relationship becomes and the more willing everyone is to provide the customer with a little something extra that starts to erode profit. Worse yet is that the longtime customer often continues to receive a lower price, which obviously results in an immediate loss of profit.

To calculate PSF, consider the following worksheet, which I've populated with sample data:

Year 1 Projected Profit:	$7,000
Cost of Initial Sale:	$6,000
Customer's Year 1 Profit/Loss:	$1,000

Annual Customer Profit:	$7,000
Annual Cost of Maintaining the Customer (Sales and Customer Service):	$2,000
Net Profit (Customer Profit Minus Cost of Maintaining):	$5,000
Probability of Keeping the Customer:	90%
Profitability Sustainability Factor:	**$4,500**

(Net Profit Multiplied by Probability of Keeping the Customer)

When determining the cost of the initial sale, be sure to include all of the costs associated with the sales and marketing process. Too many times companies overlook what they spend on annual marketing programs as part of the cost of acquiring business. At the same time, salespeople also fail to realize the number of hours they devote to closing one sale. This happens most often when the first sales call goes well and salespeople are lulled into the belief that they'll be able to close the sale quickly, only to run into numerous obstacles when they try to close the actual deal. In fact, this is one of the reasons I've written this book—to help salespeople shorten the selling cycle so that they can earn more profit on each sale.

A Big Order at the Wrong Price Isn't Worth It

I remember well how excited I was when, as a new salesperson for a major company, I closed what I thought was a significant sale with a difficult customer. I truly believed my hard work, compelling story, great presentation, and superior communication skills had helped me secure a great sale.

Sure, I got the order. However, what I failed to realize was how the customer had skillfully given me the order in a way that wound up costing my company a significant sum of money. Although it was a very large order, I had agreed that my company would cover the cost of shipping the product and moving it all the way through the customer's supply chain. At the time, I thought that what the customer was asking for was reasonable. It all sounded logical, considering the size of the order. There was no way it couldn't help but make a lot of money for my company, right? *Wrong.*

Several months after the sale, I began to realize what the order had actually cost us and how little profit we ultimately made. The lesson I learned, painfully, was that we would have made more money if I had not sold the customer as large an order. Because I allowed myself to get caught up in the emotional excitement of a huge order, the customer—who was much more experienced—took me to the cleaners.

The only thing I'm proud of with regard to this sale is the fact that it occurred early in my sales career and I was able to learn from it. I tell this story because not only does it provide an example of how easy it is for a salesperson to give up profit, but it also sheds light on the concept of "intellectual profit." I learned something from my mistake and was able to use the information to improve my selling ability. Had I not done anything with the information I learned in terms of making myself a better salesperson, then there would have been no intellectual profit on the sale.

Keep in mind that intellectual profit might be great, but it doesn't put food on your table or clothes on your children until it's turned into real profit. If you can't turn a financial profit on what you are selling, then all the intellectual profit in the world isn't going to help you. The best use of intellectual profitability is when you take what you learn from one sale and apply it to the next sale. When I work with sales managers, I always tell them to make sure they challenge their salespeople at the end of each day to reflect on what they learned about their sales process and how they can use that newfound knowledge to improve their sales process tomorrow.

There's not a salesperson out there who hasn't had an experience similar to what I went through early in my career that resulted in losing profit. The single greatest lesson you should take away from this book is that you need to remain focused on profit during every single sales call. When your company earns a profit, it is able to reinvest that profit into other things the company has deemed to be a priority. Profit is the fuel that allows you and your company to achieve even greater accomplishments. Profit is everything.

Intellectual Profitability Adds Up

In the previous story I shared how I was able to earn some intellectual profitability. It's worth repeating that intellectual profitability is not something you can use to feed your children, but it can make a significant difference in the amount of profit you can create for yourself and your company over the long term.

I'm a proponent of the term "intellectual profitability" because I firmly believe the vast majority of companies underestimate the importance of you—*the salesperson*. The greater your intellectual profitability, the greater the contribution you'll make to your company. There's a fundamental rule that says nothing a company makes or provides is a sustainable competitive advantage over the long term. There will always be someone else who can make or provide what you do now, only do it better, faster, or cheaper.

That being the case, the only sustainable competitive advantage any company can have in the long run is the people it employs and the intellectual capacity those people are able to contribute. Your intellectual profitability is crucial! Just like an investment that grows over time due to compounding interest, your intellectual profitability has the ability to grow through the compounding of your sales experience.

Early in this chapter I pointed out that there are two types of intellectual profitability from which the salesperson can benefit. Areas where intellectual profitability plays a significant role are managing major accounts and dealing with complex negotiation situations. The higher the level of intellectual profitability you have, the more profitable the major account will be and the more success you'll have negotiating outcomes.

If you are a sales manager, pay close attention to intellectual profit. As a sales manager, it's your responsibility to help your salespeople grow. Therefore, it's important for you to know how to measure intellectual profit. The best way to measure it is by regularly asking your salespeople what they've learned from their customers and how they're using that knowledge—not just with the customer they learned it from, but with all of their customers.

If you are in a service-driven business, intellectual profit is critical. For salespeople in this area, many times selling is driven by proprietary knowledge and the ability to use it to create insights the customer can benefit from. If you sell commodites the issue of intellectual profit is still important, but it takes on a slightly different twist and is more customer-driven. Because the goal is selling commodities, most information is more readily available to everyone in the industry. Intellectual profit therefore needs to be centered around the customer's needs.

The challenge in both cases is in understanding what has value and what does not have value to the customer. Just ask yourself this question: *How can I use what I just learned to improve my sales process and customer profitability?* It's not rocket science. In fact, I encourage people to keep it simple, because otherwise it's too easy to get caught up in looking for intellectual profit. As I said earlier, intellectual profit is great, but it doesn't always put food on the table when you need it most.

Minimize the Profit Takers

Every salesperson and company has to be aware that they probably have customers that are either not profitable or less profitable than the average customer. Salespeople and sales managers are always quick to point out what they believe are profitable customers. However, in many cases, once-profitable customers can later reach a point where they are generating minimal profit or, worse yet, taking profit out of your company.

The challenge here is that salespeople and management often will try to justify keeping these customers. They will claim it doesn't make sense to cut low-profit customers because of the pending growth they expect to get from them, or they'll be under some mythical perception that although these customers are not profitable, they are at least generating great cash flow. These kinds of reasons can cloud people's judgment and ultimately eat away at the company's profits. This philosophy also takes away valuable sales time that could be better spent in other areas.

Don't try to justify a low-profit customer or, even worse, a profit-loss customer. The sooner you deal with it, the better. The customer that's hurting your bottom-line profit is often hurting your operations in numerous other ways that don't show up on the profit line. The low-profit customer is often the same customer that is always making demands on customer service, logistics, and operations. You do not want to be an organization that just deals with these requests, all the while ignoring the true costs to your bottom line.

The easiest way to deal with the low-profit customer is by being up-front with them and implementing a price increase. Don't waffle about it. Do it! Tell the customer what the new pricing is going to be and then let the customer make the decision of either paying the higher price or walking away. If these customers walk away, you win. You now have resources you can devote to higher-profit customers. If they continue with you and pay the higher amount, then you've just corrected the problem and are now receiving the profit that correlates with what you are providing. In this case, too, you win. The only way you don't win is if you choose to do nothing and merely rationalize away the bad decision to keep the customer at an insufficient profit margin.

"Profit" Is a Beautiful Word

Profit is what you must keep in the forefront of your mind each time you make a sales call. It's profit that allows a company to determine if a salesperson deserves more compensation. It's profit that determines how and where a company should grow. It's profit that ultimately gives you, the salesperson, confidence that the company you work for today is going to be around tomorrow.

If "profit" were such a dirty word, there wouldn't be so many customers asking to see a company's financials before doing business with a new vendor. Many customers want to ensure that the vendor they are considering forming a relationship with has the financial stability to provide the products and service they need—not just now, but over the long term. There's nothing more frustrating for a customer than to begin sourcing critical components from a vendor only to have that supplier go out of business and leave the customer unable to serve its own customers. Just take a few minutes to read up on any of the numerous stories about critical manufacturing sectors being shut down due to the financial collapse of a key supplier. If you are in a business where your customers would view you as a critical supplier, you must be prepared to leverage your profitability both in the short and long term.

Profit is beautiful. The sooner everyone accepts it as being beautiful and a critical component of a business's success, the better off both you and the customer are. You both can focus on getting done what needs to get done.

CHAPTER 3

Use Needs and Benefits to Command a Higher Price

UNDERSTANDING WHY PEOPLE buy is a science in and of itself. For the typical salesperson, the problem is that there just isn't enough time in a day to turn the sales process into a science laboratory test. You need to close the sale. However, if you don't understand why the customer is buying, then you run the risk of your sales process being nothing more than an exercise in customer service. The sales process is about creating sales that otherwise would not have been made, for quantities that otherwise would not have been bought, at a price that is higher than typically would have been secured. Let me explain.

When a salesperson receives an order that was going to be placed anyway, I honestly can't call that "selling." That's just giving good customer service. If customers buy only what they had originally planned to purchase, again, I call that "customer service." Finally, if customers pay what they expected to pay or less, then that, too, is customer service. Your role as a salesperson is to uncover the customer's needs and desired benefits and then, equipped with this knowledge, close the sale.

Far too often a sale is made at a price point far lower than what salespeople could have received if only they had been patient enough to uncover the customer's real needs. It's my belief that although customers may be satisfied with the purchase they just made, they would have been just as happy or even happier paying more if the salesperson had been able to draw out of them what they *really* needed and wanted.

While the reasons for lowering price are varied, at the top of the list is the desire of many salespeople to close the sale as quickly as possible. On the surface, there may not be anything wrong with trying to close a sale early, but too often a speedy close means that salespeople won't be able to get the price they really need to achieve the profit margin their company expects. Closing the sale early may deliver volume, but if it doesn't deliver as much profit as is possible, then volume means very little.

In *Slow Down, Sell Faster* (AMACOM, 2011), Kevin Davis does a great job of pointing out the dangers of closing a sale too fast, and I highly recommend that everyone who reads this book read his book as well. When you sell without fully understanding the customer's needs, you not only lose out on profit with *that* sale, but you also limit your ability to generate the next sale.

Maximizing your sales profit means maximizing your sales process, too. There's no better way to do that than by closing each sale in a way that automatically opens the door to the next sale. And the best way to start is to make sure your first sale is completed in a manner that allows you to fully understand the needs the customer has and the benefits the customer desires.

Chasing the Shiny Object

A few years ago, my wife and I were in the market to buy a new car. We live in an area of the country that gets a fair amount of snowfall, and having never owned a sports utility vehicle, we decided that a four-wheel drive probably made sense. This, then, was one of the needs we wanted to fulfill when we went shopping.

We were amazed that once a seller learned that we were interested in a four-wheel-drive SUV, every dealership we visited, and every salesperson with whom we spoke, steered the conversation toward the merits of a four-wheel drive. They went on endlessly about how it would allow my wife (who would be the primary driver) to navigate around town regardless of weather conditions. This was all good and fine, but not one salesperson explored any other benefits that also could have been important to us had those benefits been brought to our attention.

As I mentioned in Chapter 2, this is what I call "chasing the shiny object." A salesperson hears something and immediately begins making assumptions about what it means. Every salesperson assumed that what was of primary importance to my wife was four-wheel drive, when in fact that was just *one* of the needs she had. She also wanted a car with a great sound system and heated comfortable seats. These two benefits were almost more important to her, despite the probability of having to drive on snow-covered roads. The salespeople could have closed the sale a lot sooner had they explored everything my wife was looking for. There were several SUVs we could have purchased, including some that had what we considered secondary benefits of being stylish and black. In the end, we bought an SUV with four-wheel-drive system that also had comfortable heated seats and an upgraded sound system.

What I found funny about the entire sales process was that it took a lot longer than it needed to. The salespeople with whom we dealt were focused on one need, which actually was not our highest priority. When they couldn't close, they began chasing us on price, which obviously was to our advantage. If they had done a better job of finding out our needs and the benefits we desired earlier in the sales process, they likely could have closed the sale sooner and at a higher price.

Determining the Customer's Needs and Benefits

The sales process involves a number of activities, but at the top of the list is uncovering the customer's actual needs and desired benefits. The process is pretty straightforward. The more you understand your customer, the more opportunities you'll have to maximize the profit you make from the sale. The question is: Why aren't more salespeople successful in uncovering what their customers want and then maximizing the profit opportunity?

I believe the reason is simple: Salespeople know their products and services too well, and as a result they focus too heavily on features. Making matters worse, they then *assume* that customers can quickly grasp how the features will satisfy their needs. Salespeople hate it when the customer starts viewing the product as nothing more than a commodity or something that can be easily compared to another product, but that is exactly what happens when the discussion is about product features and not benefits. When customers only see the features, then it is natural for them to turn their attention to comparing your offering to other offerings they've seen. At that point in the sales process, it becomes nothing more than a game of the lowest price getting the order. No wonder salespeople think too many customers focus only on price; they've led the customers there themselves. Usually this problem can be eliminated if salespeople take the time to discuss benefits rather than focusing on the features of what they are selling.

The salesperson's inability or unwillingness to focus on the customer's needs and wants is what compels the salesperson to request a price reduction from her company. I bring up this issue throughout the book because it's such a significant problem. As I mentioned right up front in Chapter 1, any time salespeople are not successful, they will always say price is the reason they didn't close a sale. You don't think they are going to admit that they weren't able to close the sale because of their own ineptness, do you? There's no reason for a sales manager, marketing manager, or anyone else to ever respond to a salesperson's plea for a discount or other economic incentive without first asking the salesperson the following three questions:

1. What are the needs of the customer? (There must always be at least three needs, and price cannot be one of them.)

2. What did the customer say that leads you to believe these are his needs?

3. What approach did you take to closing the sale, and what was the customer's response?

These same questions are what every salesperson should ask herself after every sales call that does not result in a sale. If you are willing to ask yourself these questions on a regular basis, answer them truthfully, and subsequently improve your sales process, I guarantee you will improve both your rate of closing and, more important, the profitability of each sale.

You'll notice that I emphasize that the salesperson must identify at least three customer needs, and that price cannot be one of them. In my years working with sales teams, I've found three to be the minimum, and that identifying six customer needs is an even better goal. The more needs you uncover, the more profitable the sale can be for both you and the customer. (Remember, customers receive profit from buying something when that product or service satisfies their needs. It only stands to reason, then, that the more needs your customers have, the more money they will be willing to pay to have them met.)

A salesperson needs to have at least three needs to discuss with the customer to keep the discussion from defaulting back to price. By uncovering three or more needs or benefits that the customer desires, you gain enough flexibility to not only craft a profitable sales proposal for the customer, but also to start laying the framework for your next sale.

Be honest and ask yourself how many times you have closed a sale without really knowing your customers' needs and the benefits they're looking for. I admit that I've done it far too many times. The reason is that we rush. We see the chance to close and don't want to miss out on it, for fear that the sale will be lost forever.

Let's start digging deeper into finding at least three of the customer's needs and/or the benefits the customer desires. The definition I use: *Something is not a need or a benefit until the customer tells me it's a need or benefit.* One of the biggest problems salespeople have is the tendency to reach conclusions based on their own perceptions instead of accurate information provided by the customer.

Customers have their needs and desire certain benefits, but not all needs and benefits are created equal. You need to uncover the primary needs and benefits that will allow you to gain the information you need to close the sale profitably for the customer, yourself, and your company.

Let's return to the story I shared earlier. When my wife and I wanted to purchase a new car, nearly every salesperson believed that our primary need was for a four-wheel-drive vehicle to get us through winter weather. Bad assumption. Why? Although four-wheel drive was indeed a need, it was not our only need. Yet the salesperson never engaged us to talk about what we wanted in a new car. On a couple of occasions the salesperson didn't even offer us a chance to talk, opting instead to do all of the talking. That's why it is important for the salesperson to listen to and hear, in the customer's own words, what the customer needs and desires.

Customers who feel strongly about a certain need will want to talk about it, with and without the salesperson's prompting. If you listen closely, you can pick up on clues that indicate something is especially important to a customer. First, however, you must be able to make the customer feel comfortable and willing to share information. Second—which is really part of the first point—you need to ask questions that allow customers to fully express what they want.

And by the way, although the goal is to uncover the customer's primary needs and desired benefits, the astute salesperson knows that customers often have additional needs and desired benefits in mind, too. I refer to them as "secondary needs and benefits," because they may not be essential but are still important to the customer. Understanding them can help open the door for a second sale. Never ignore any secondary needs or benefits. The ability to use them at a later time can be the difference in making a future sale a profitable sale.

Separating Good Information from Bad

Customers are not going to share with you information that's not important to them. They just won't. That doesn't mean, though, that all information a customer shares with you is good information. Customers will only share with a salesperson two types of information: good information that helps you understand their needs and information to distract you. Yes, customers will provide information to distract you. They do this because they fear they are losing control and you, as the salesperson, may have the advantage of knowing too much about what customers want, so they may wield information to regain control. Customers also use this tactic to try and get you to think that they won't pay the asking price. This tactic is especially common early in the sales process, when the customer does not yet have a level of confidence in the salesperson.

The challenge is for you to understand what is good information and what is bad information designed to distract you. This is why I'm a firm believer that everything the customer says should prompt you to ask follow-up questions to determine the *quality* of the information the customer has provided. I also strongly recommend asking follow-up questions later in your sales call, in order to better assess the information the customer may have shared with you at the beginning of the sales call. This way you can quickly determine if what the customer was sharing was good information or something to distract you into believing something else. If the information was important, the customer will still want to talk about it, which then allows you to begin to determine if it is a primary or secondary need. Customers who only discuss certain needs or benefits when prompted by the salesperson are most likely sharing secondary needs. The needs or desired benefits they bring up without your prompting are most likely to be primary needs.

No matter what phase of the sales process you are in, you need to listen carefully to be sure that what you are hearing from your customers is good information. Although customers are less likely to offer up misleading information when they are about ready to close the sale, it can still happen. Customers will sometimes give you bad information at the end of the sale as a way to suddenly try and get a lower price. Again, the way to get the discussion back on track is to always ask your customers a question that gets them to describe the number one benefit or need they are looking for the product or service to meet. Immediately after they answer the question, you should then ask for the sale. Typically, customers who attempt to distract salespeople just as they are about to close have only one goal in mind—to get a lower price. Salespeople who are not confident will fall for this tactic and offer a discount. Confident salespeople will leverage what their customers have told them about their needs and their desired benefits and use the information to close the sale.

What We Can Learn About Needs and Benefits from Apple

Apple Inc. is an example of a company that has successfully launched new devices that consumers didn't know they needed until Apple introduced them. Look at any Apple product without knowing anything about how you could benefit from it and you would quickly surmise that the product is high priced, especially when compared to other, similar devices by competing companies. However, a loyal Apple customer would say they are quite reasonably priced products, considering all the things Apple devices can do. Right there is the sweet spot of what I'm talking about. The non-Apple user perceives Apple products as being expensive. The Apple fanatic sees the devices as being a bargain. It comes down to what the customer sees as value, based on the customer's needs or the benefits the customer desires.

When Apple comes out with a new device, it goes through an education process with consumers to get them to see the wide range of benefits the device offers. Early technology adopters or Apple fanatics are naturally the first to respond, but, in time, hordes of consumers begin flocking to purchase and use the new device. In each case, consumers buy based on what they see as their primary need and then in time they begin to see value in other secondary benefits they didn't initially appreciate. The iPhone is a great example of this. When it was first released people saw it as an expensive phone, not realizing everything it could do. Over time, as consumers became more familiar with the iPhone they began to see all of the secondary benefits it had to offer. For many buyers of the iPhone it was the secondary benefits that quickly made the iPhone so valuable to them, giving them confidence to buy another Apple product. This is why I'm a very strong believer that any salesperson making a sale needs to uncover both the primary and secondary needs of the customer.

Using Follow-Up Questions to Categorize a Customer's Needs

When customers are sharing their needs with you, it is absolutely essential to ask them follow-up questions. The depth of information they share with you is what you can use to determine if their need is primary or secondary.

In situations where customers may have difficulty explaining their needs, your success in making the sale may come down to your ability to ask questions. You cannot take the shortcut of drawing your own conclusions and putting words in the customer's mouth. If you do, you run the risk of having the customer lose confidence in you, which ultimately will come back to bite you when you attempt to close the sale. Let your customers talk. You can guide them along with your questions. A few questions I like to use include "How would you see yourself using this?" "Could you explain more?" and "Why do you feel that way?" Your ability to close the sale at a higher margin is more likely when you allow them to fully express their needs and the benefits they desire in their own words.

Needs? Benefits? What's the Difference, Anyway?

Throughout this chapter, I've been using two words a lot—*needs* and *benefits*. I've used them in several different ways, but almost always together. Does this mean the two words share the same meaning? Yes and no. Yes, they share the same meaning in the context of being things that the customer is looking for: Customers have needs that they want a product or service to meet, and they desire benefits from the products or services they purchase. However, "needs" convey a higher sense of urgency than "benefits." Before you start disagreeing with me, let me explain.

When I hear the word *need,* I think of something that has to be fulfilled, and relatively soon. An example might be my need to travel to Europe next month for business. A *benefit* is something I'll gain from my trip to Europe. The primary benefit I want by traveling to Europe is to be able to participate in an upcoming sales conference. A secondary benefit is being able to meet people I didn't expect to see. Furthermore, if I fail to fulfill my *need* to travel to Europe, there is no way I can expect to fulfill my other benefits. Although the primary benefit is being at the sales conference, over time the secondary benefit of meeting new people may become even bigger.

The amount of money I would be willing to pay to make this trip is going to be equal to the amount of value I expect to get from the trip. I may very well choose to participate in this sales conference again next year if I believe either the primary need of being there is still as important or the secondary benefit of meeting people has increased in value. Over the course of a few years, it could very well be that the secondary benefit of meeting people winds up becoming the primary benefit.

In this example, you can begin to see how *needs* are generally those things we have to have. Additionally, needs usually have an element of timeliness associated with them. *Benefits* are those things we'll gain once the need is met. You may beg to differ with me based on textbooks you've read and what you've been taught in a sales program. I'm fine with that; however, let me share with you my reasoning. First, all sales are time-driven. Any sale that does not have the element of time associated with it has no chance of ever being maximized for profit. This is especially true when it comes to negotiating. There is little chance of success in any negotiation if there is not an element of time. When we introduce a time frame into a sale, it allows both the salesperson and the customer to begin associating a dollar value with the sale. No sale can ever be completed if there is not a dollar value connected with it.

Benefits, on the other hand, may or may not have time associated with them. However, a benefit definitely has to have a gain connected with it, which is a gain the customer will be able to realize by making the purchase. Here, then, are two more of my rules:

1. Needs are most likely all primary.

2. Benefits can be either primary or secondary.

When asking the customer questions, ask questions that are centered on needs first, to help you understand their value to the customer and to give you an indication of the customer's buying time frame. There is nothing worse than being in a sales discussion with customers talking about the benefits they desire, only to find out they have little interest in buying for another year. That's the moment, in fact, when a lot of salespeople begin falling into the price discount trap. They've spent considerable time with the customer uncovering primary and secondary benefits, only to find out there is no sense of urgency on the customer's part to buy. If you are the salesperson, suddenly you believe that if you put a discounted price in front of the customer, you can somehow get the customer to buy now. The problem, then, is the customer often reacts to the discount and makes the purchase. Victory, right? Not exactly.

Salespeople go away thinking they pulled off a major coup by being able to turn a nonsale into a sale. In reality, all they did was get a sale. Unfortunately, they didn't do it at the maximum profit, which is the central theme of this book. The only profit they can say they maximized was their own time, but even this came at a high cost. Not only did the salesperson not get as much profit as was possible, but the customer now has a newfound perception of having his needs and benefits met at a lower price.

Over time this becomes a real issue with salespeople. Left unchecked, salespeople will focus their entire selling process on uncovering benefits, rather than first exploring the customer's needs.

Since needs are so important, let's take a moment to explain how to leverage them. Early in the process, your questions need to establish the customer's intended timeline to purchase. Yes, if you are dealing with a professional buyer or someone who loves to manipulate salespeople, there can be some serious game-playing. For example, a buyer may say that she is not looking to make a purchase for at least two more years. This is a good example of a customer throwing out bad information. When someone shares with you an unrealistic time frame you have to consider that the person may be bluffing. The information the customer shared may indeed not be the timeline. If you fall for the customer's game of "delaying buying," you may easily find yourself in the price discount game as well.

I've been in situations involving large business-to-business transactions where buyers have stated from the get-go that they are not looking to make a purchase for at least three years. In one situation in particular, another salesperson and I decided to call the customer out on this. When we got up to leave, saying we'd check back with the customer in six to nine months, the customer stopped us and admitted that he most likely would be buying as soon as corporate gave its approval. Surprising how the customer's tone changed when we called his bluff. (I should add that we never made a sale with this customer; in fact, we made the decision to walk away from the customer based on the customer's buying process. We learned very quickly the customer was giving us diversionary information. In several follow-up calls, the customer continued to share with us information that was misleading, leaving us with no way to develop the level of confidence necessary to create a profitable sale.)

Understanding the customer's need to buy is critical, and the more you can link such needs to a timeline, the better. I also recommend that you come right out and ask your customers why they are looking to buy. You'll be surprised at what information your customers will share with you. Just remember that you need to verify whatever your customers tell you. You do that by listening to them closely: Are they telling you the same things again at a point later in the sales call or during a follow-up call? How customers respond to your follow-up questions will allow you to discern if their need is real and/or if it is a primary or secondary benefit.

I also don't hesitate to ask customers how they've made similar purchases in the past. This line of questioning is a way to uncover if there are other people who should be involved in the sales process. Often when people are asked this question, they'll mention the name of someone else in the company who has handled other buying decisions. This naturally sends a strong signal that the person with whom you are speaking is not the primary decision maker. People who are not primary decision makers are usually more driven to try to leverage a price discount. Why? Typically, only the primary decision maker truly understands the full benefit of the future purchase—and the merits of paying a full price for it. If, on the other hand, you are attempting to sell to someone who is not the primary decision maker, that person probably will not understand the full value and will instead focus on securing a lower price as a measure of what's most important in the buying process.

When I talk about maximizing profit by maximizing the price, it all comes down to being able to truly determine the customer's needs and desired benefits. Sometimes customers will easily share information about what they need and want. Other times, they may be far more hesitant. In either case, remember this: Something is not a true need or benefit you can leverage until the customer has expressed it to you more than once. That's why you must keep asking follow-up questions to verify the quality of the information you are getting from your customer. The key to determining if the customer's stated need is primary or secondary can be found in how frequently the customer wants to talk about it. Primary needs and benefits will naturally be those items the customer talks about the most. In every case, you must use the information not only to help close the first sale at a higher profit margin, but also to begin setting up the next sale.

Failure to determine a customer's needs and desired benefits can result in your having to discount your price to close the sale. When you discount your price, the only thing you are doing is creating volume, but the result is actually a loss in profit. In the end, no amount of volume can offset the profit you missed out on by not selling at full price.

Creating Real Value Using Your Price Point

EVERYBODY WANTS A DISCOUNT, and it seems that too many businesses and salespeople are more than happy to accommodate by offering a lower price. It all comes down to "pricing perception" and what I believe is an "over conditioning" of the consumer. In both business-to-consumer and business-to-business transactions, customers have come to expect a discount. This chapter describes what it takes to develop a pricing perception with the customer that allows you to maximize profits. Mastering these skills enables companies and salespeople to build a high-margin business without having to discount.

The *Wall Street Journal* regularly reports on companies that have just signed off on a major sale. The selling company is pleased to simply announce the new sale, while the purchasing company is satisfied only if the news article states that it was able to achieve some significant discount. ("Look at what a great deal we got!") Deals between one of the major aircraft manufacturers and airlines or aircraft-leasing companies are typical. After reading the article, you are left wondering what the price is and what the value is. In this case, the real value is something only the airline or leasing company purchasing the aircraft need to be concerned about.

Forming Real Value Around Price

Forming real value around a price is tricky because what you believe it should be as a salesperson and what the customer believes it should be as a buyer are often worlds apart. For example, consider someone who sells actual businesses. The business broker knows only too well the problem of forming real value. If a business broker is attempting to sell a small business, the current owners probably have put a lifetime of sweat and heart into that business, so you can guess how they will see their business valued. The business owner will expect a significantly higher amount than the person who is looking to buy the business is ready to offer. This is only natural. Perceived value is just that—it is *perceived*. It's what we believe individually as a salesperson and as a customer.

Creating perceived value is centered on understanding the needs of customers and the benefits they want, as discussed at length in Chapter 3. What I am going to talk about now is how to structure the price point itself in a manner that allows it to have value. It's really quite easy to do, yet for some reason, few salespeople and companies take advantage of this method, let alone maximize the potential that can come from creating price-point perception.

One reason I believe companies do not take full advantage of this method is because they have attempted to streamline their operations for the sake of efficiency. In so doing, they have altered the perception of what customers think of them. Specifically, I'm talking about how companies, in an attempt to improve their overall margins, have discontinued entire product lines or numerous individual items that had low sales but potentially high profit margins. From an operations perspective, you obviously can see it is one of the best things any company can do to improve its bottom line. Essentially, the company eliminates slow-moving items. However, what ends up happening is that all this streamlining also can change significantly how customers perceive the products and the company. Let's look at how this works.

Creating the Price Point

If you are selling a line of products, chances are you have multiple offerings from which the customer can pick. Some of the items you offer are going to be priced higher while other items will be priced lower. You know in your mind why they are priced this way, based on how much the items cost to make and the benefits the customer is going to receive from them. What most salespeople tend to forget is the quick comparison customers will do anytime they are offered several price points. As much as you'd like to think that customers will grasp the inherent differences in the items, more likely than not they are gravitating toward the price point. Running through their minds are some quick assumptions as to what the price points are saying.

In other words, customers are subconsciously making decisions that they likely will never share with you, the salesperson. Yes, you can ask your customers what they think of the price points, but that is not something I would recommend. Your discussion will drift off course to talking about price alone, long before you want it to head in this direction. The natural option is, of course, to not show the customer any price points until just before you are about to close. This is my preferred strategy. However, for those customers who insist on discussing price before you can at least trial close, I suggest the following strategy: Offer the customer your ultra-price package.

The Power of the Ultra-Price Package

For the customer who demands you talk price early in the sales call, always have available and be ready to share what I call the "ultra-price package." This is the absolute highest price offering you and your company can assemble. Load it up with everything. Make sure it includes every service imaginable and then some. The key is to have the absolute price point be much higher than you would ever expect a customer to accept. Just in case you have a customer who does want the ultra-price package, make sure you can deliver on it, and make sure the offering is packed with the added value and benefits that warrant the high price. By the way, maximizing your profit margin with the ultra-price package is an absolute must. Even if you don't expect customers to ever buy it, that doesn't mean you should do things to reduce your margin. This is where companies that cut out all items except their bestsellers end up hurting themselves. Not having the "ultra-price" item prevents them from being able to contrast high prices with what I'll call their more "normal" prices.

When you show the customer the ultra-price package, you are going to draw a reaction. That is exactly what you want—a reaction. Most likely, customers will tell you that the price is much more than what they were expecting to pay. This is the reaction you want, because whether customers even realize it in that moment, their mind is already being conditioned by a higher price. By showing them the ultra-price package, you are now in a position where whatever your next tier of pricing is, customers will view it as being a bargain. This is true even if the price you now show them is simply your *normal* full-price offering.

If you doubt how well this method works, then you need look no further than how consulting firms price their services or how retailers merchandise. Consulting firms, as you can imagine, are in the business of selling intellectual insights. As a result, their pricing can vary dramatically based on the perceived value of what the customer is going to gain. In any initial meeting, a consulting firm is always going to offer up the maximum price or, as consultants might say, the "investment" amount. They do so primarily to gauge the customer's reaction. By creating the perception of high price, they begin to affect what the customer may have been expecting to pay prior to the meeting. In a very short period, the consulting firm has taken the customer from one expectation up to a much higher expectation. Does this method still require the salesperson to sell? It sure does, but now the salespeople are able to build their value proposition around a higher perceived value without having to go through a slow-motion process. That slow-motion process is what I refer to as "working the customer up the pricing ladder." It may eventually work, but a quicker approach is to build higher perceived value on the front end.

Many times retailers will do the same thing when they merchandise. For example, in the center of a display of women's purses and handbags, the retailer may place a purse that is much more expensive than what average shopper would pay. But then the retailer will surround this purse with lower-priced purses of the same brand. Suddenly, the lower-priced purses seem to be a bargain, even though they are not discounted at all.

The real beauty of having an ultra-price package you can share with customers is that every now and then, you will find a customer who wants it. When this happens, you are suddenly—and fortunately—in a position of being able to maximize your price and your profit. When you do have customers who respond favorably to the ultra-price package, don't lose the sale by showing shock that they want it. Be fully prepared to communicate to customers exactly what they are getting for their money. If you are going to present an ultra-price offering, you must also believe in it and be ready to respond favorably if and when a customer responds favorably to it.

There is another significant benefit that salespeople will realize when they fully appreciate the value of the ultra-price package. They will increase their own level of price-point expectations. Just as customers' perception is changed when they see a price point far higher than they were expecting, so too does the salesperson's perception change. Salespeople who get in the habit of offering their customers the ultra-price offering will begin to see everything else they offer as being an absolute bargain, certainly not worthy of any type of discounting.

Ultra-Prices and a Salesperson's Beliefs

In my work as a sales consultant, I've worked with clients to put in place an ultra-price offering for the sole purpose of helping recondition the sales force to become more comfortable with the client's normal, full-price offerings. In each case where this strategy was executed, it succeeded more than the client ever thought possible. Additionally, in each case, the client made sales at the ultra-price. Just remember, if you are going to use this type of strategy, you must be prepared to deliver at all levels of the company.

Some of you may be asking, "If this strategy is so good, why don't more companies and salespeople use it?" I believe it is because they are afraid of a customer getting upset when presented with the ultra-price package. If that's the case, I would argue that the issue is not with the ultra-price package.

Rather, the problem is with the salesperson not being confident enough during the selling process. If your salespeople cannot enter into a discussion with a customer and be confident about what they are offering and the benefits they can provide to the customer, then why are they in the selling profession? I've worked with clients who have been hesitant to employ this strategy, and in my experience it comes down to this very problem.

Salespeople who lack confidence in what they are selling are going to rely on price discounting as their primary strategy to secure sales, or they will capture only those sales that literally fall into their lap. Either way, they should not be called "salespeople." I shouldn't have to point this out, but they also have little chance of ever being able to maximize the profit potential for themselves and their company.

The "No Negotiation" Philosophy

Another great sales strategy you can use to secure full price and profit is to have the policy of not negotiating with a customer over anything that could negatively affect your profit. This strategy is very powerful once the sales force accepts the role it plays. Another expression I like to use is, "Sell first. Negotiate second." In other words, if you do a good job of selling—if you truly listen to what your customers need and want and then align your offering to them—you have a very good opportunity to close the sale. Too many salespeople allow themselves to get drawn into the negotiation phase before they have been able to identify, at the minimum, three of the customer's needs or desired benefits. (Remember, identify-ing as many as six customer needs is the better goal.)

Aggressive customers often will attempt to get the salesperson to begin negotiating early on in the sales process. They do this because they believe it will give them the upper hand in being able to secure a lower price later on. Typically, in these situations, the customer is successful because the salesperson becomes scared about losing the sale if negotia-tions don't start right away. Unfortunately, when this occurs, not only does the salesperson lose out on profit with the sale, but the customer now has a lower price-to-value perception of what the salesperson is selling. The customer will expect this lower price on all sales going forward. As you can see, the damage shows up in the loss of short-term profit *and* long-term profit.

As bad as it is to lose profit, the bigger problem comes into play with each and every future customer the salesper-son interacts with. Once one customer is able to get the salesperson to negotiate early, the next customer will find it even easier to leverage such techniques. This is true even if the two customers have never talked to each other! Once the confidence of the salesperson has been compromised, the salesperson will be more likely to entertain negotiations prematurely again. Before you know it, the salesperson has developed a new bad habit of giving away profit by entering into negotiations with a customer too early in the selling process. I cannot emphasize it enough: *Sell first. Negotiate second.*

Sales Managers: Don't Empower Salespeople to Give Away Profit

Another way profit is compromised is when the salesperson has the green light to adjust pricing on the spot, without having to secure approval from anyone else. When salespeople have this leeway, they may feel empowered and much more capable of closing a sale. In reality, though, they have been empowered only with the ability to give away profit. Salespeople who are able to discount a price at their own discretion will always do so more frequently than salespeople who cannot discount a price without first gaining approval from their manager.

The "no negotiation" policy is black-and-white. It says the salesperson does not have the ability to reduce or alter the pricing in any manner, period. The policy only works if it is applied without exception 100 percent of the time. You cannot have the policy with certain customers but not with other customers. If you have an inconsistent policy, the salesperson will essentially become a split personality and, over time, won't be able to close sales with either customer group.

I guarantee that if you are a sales manager and you firmly institute the "no negotiation" policy with a sales team that, up till now, has had the freedom to negotiate prices, you will receive significant pushback. If you are the sales manager implementing the policy, you'll hear every reason imaginable as to why it won't work. You also will hear complaints that you are no longer allowing salespeople to sell, but rather are turning them into nothing more than order takers. Senior salespeople may even threaten that you are forcing them to quit or may suggest that you are giving a lot of sales away to the competition. I have heard all of these arguments on a number of occasions. Trust me—the "no negotiation" policy works no matter what your salespeople say.

There are, however, situations where this policy will not work. First, don't look to implement the policy if you are in an industry where what you sell is a commodity and there are many suppliers. Second, do not attempt to implement the policy in those industries where customers expect a bidding process or, worse yet, a reverse auction. The only way you can use the "no negotiation" policy in these types of situations is if you have enough added-value services and options for which your customers have expressed a need.

Where Does the "No Negotiation" Policy Work Best?

The "no negotiation" policy works best in industries where you have time to execute the selling process and can determine the customer's real needs and desired benefits, or where you at least have the option of altering your go-to market strategy to allow more selling time to maximize your profit potential. It also works well in industries where customers are not pressed to make a decision, or the decision they may end up making is to not buy from you and stay with their existing supplier as a way of not having to make a decision. The final criterion is that the company using the "no negotiation" policy must have offerings that allow it to distinguish itself from the competition.

Examples of industries that fit these criteria are those of a service nature or with a high level of value-added services associated with the products the customer is purchasing. Surprisingly, there are more industries that fit this description than you may initially realize, including healthcare, consulting services, financial services, technology, and even software, to name only a few. If your industry fits the criteria outlined, then you have a very high probability of being able to successfully implement this strategy.

Rules for an Effective "No Negotiation" Policy

Once the policy is implemented, there are six rules to follow. If you don't adhere to them in the first few weeks after the policy is established, then there is little chance the policy will work. These rules are:

1. Management supports the policy 100 percent.
2. Everyone must understand the damage discounting does to profit.
3. Sales must understand and believe in the product offering.
4. Management and sales must be prepared to lose some sales early on.
5. Management and sales must support each other to make the policy work.

6. Management and sales must recognize and celebrate the first several times the new policy works.

Let me explain each of the rules in more detail.

Rule 1: Management Supports the Policy 100 Percent

This one may sound easy, but sometimes there are rogue sales managers who will attempt to ignore the policy. For the sake of inflating their own egos, they will offer a discount to close a sale or they will authorize their salespeople to offer discounts. Nothing will undermine the new policy faster than to have even a single manager working against the system.

Rule 2: Everyone Must Understand the Damage Discounting Does to Profit

Many salespeople fail to connect the two dots—*price* and *profit*. For some reason, they think that discounting a price does not significantly affect profit, or if there is an impact, then on a percentage basis, it won't be higher than the price discount they are offering the customer. Nothing could be further from the truth. A few calculations show that even a 10 percent reduction in price can result in a much steeper decrease in profit. Let me illustrate how much profit can be lost with just a 10 percent price discount:

Profit at Full Price

Selling Price:	$1,500
Profit:	$ 300
Profit Margin:	20.0%

Profit After Discount

10% Reduction in Price:	$ 150
New Discounted Price:	$1,350
New Profit:	$ 150
Profit Margin:	11.1%
Reduction in Profit:	50.0%

In this example, a simple 10 percent reduction in price resulted in a 50 percent reduction in profit. The example above assumes there is no change in the cost of what the customer is buying at the lower price. A key item to remember is the lower the profit margin is to begin with, the greater the impact will be of any discount. If the same example used a profit margin of 50 percent ($750) before discount, then a $150 price reduction would result in only a 20 percent reduction in profit and a profit margin of 40 percent. Salespeople must understand the consequences of price discounting and carry with them the spreadsheet that allows them to calculate the effect on profit. This will give them the confidence of knowing how much damage is done when they discount.

Some of you may be saying, "Well, isn't it better to get a sale at a reduced price than no sale at all?" My answer is "No!" If you are implementing the "no negotiation" policy, then you have to be prepared to accept the fact that you will sometimes lose a sale. You must, however, keep your eye on the big picture. Using the previous example in the worksheet, you would have to double your sales just to get back to even on the profit you lost by discounting.

To really drive the point home, I tell sales managers to ask their salespeople if they would agree to double their quota for the privilege of being able to offer a 10 percent discount. Few salespeople would. Even if they would agree to such an arrangement, could your company operate, long term, doing double the volume at half the margin? Have that discussion with your operations people. They would not sign off on that proposition without taking considerable time to ramp up production.

The final argument I'll pose is this: How will your competition respond? If they'll respond by cutting their price by an equal amount, then you are right back to selling the same amount as before but now at half the margin. Have that discussion with your investors or owners. I can just see them getting ready to throw you against a wall for doing such a fine job of destroying their investment. If you are still not convinced that discounting a price can and does destroy profit, then I suggest you not bother reading the rest of the book. Focus instead on finding a job outside of sales.

Rule 3: Sales Must Understand and Believe in the Product Offering

Salespeople must understand how they can satisfy the customer's needs and desired benefits. The "no negotiation" policy works when salespeople are confident in their sales process and are capable of engaging the customer in a way that uncovers what the customer needs and wants. When companies first implement this policy, I encourage the sales team to spend time refining their sales process to ensure everyone fully understands how to leverage information the customer shares.

Rule 4: Management and Sales Must Be Prepared to Lose Some Sales Early On

Yes, it will happen. Sales will be lost. Rarely have I seen this policy implemented without some sales being lost early on. As you can imagine, the first time it occurs, everyone will begin screaming loudly about how the company is falling apart and the "no negotiation" policy is destroying the company. This response is false. The company is not falling apart, and the best way to keep that risk at bay is by establishing an aggressive new customer growth strategy at the same time the "no negotiation" policy is implemented. By putting in place an aggressive prospecting plan, salespeople and their company can minimize any early loss of sales that may occur while people are adjusting to the new policy. Remember, the number one reason salespeople discount is that they believe if they don't discount, they won't get another sale. The best way to overcome this worry is by having a full pipeline of prospects.

Rule 5: Management and Sales Must Support Each Other to Make the Policy Work

The "no negotiation" policy does not work until everyone buys into it and accepts it as the law of the land. There must be a strong level of cooperation between the two sides, and the communication must be positive. You cannot have a bunch of people whining about why something isn't working. Sales managers must behave like sales leaders.

Rule 6: Management and Sales Must Recognize and Celebrate the First Several Times the New Policy Works

Success will occur, and when it does, especially early in the process, everyone must celebrate. The reason is simple: Success creates more success. Once people begin tasting success, it will occur again and again. You must build on that momentum.

Making the "No Negotiation" Policy Work, Despite So Many Rules

If you are wondering how a "no negotiation" policy can succeed if there are so many rules to enforce, let me explain. Salespeople are naturally going to gravitate toward discounting price when they *perceive* a customer is forcing them to do it. That's human nature. It's far easier to close a sale by discounting price than it is to try and find the real benefits the customer is looking to satisfy. When you take away salespeople's ability to negotiate on price, in time they will become much more adept at asking the relevant questions that will uncover the customer's real needs and desired benefits. Over time, your salespeople will gain more confidence in their selling process and the temptation to discount will slowly go away.

Let me give you an example that may initially seem strange, but accurately illustrates my point. What do recovering alcoholics need to remain alcohol free? They have to not be exposed to alcohol. If recovering alcoholics are exposed daily to alcohol in their surroundings, it is going to be very tempting for them to slide back into their old state. If, on the other hand, they no longer are exposed to alcohol in their surroundings, then in time the temptation of alcohol becomes less and less. If you don't want to discount your price, then you must hold firm to not discounting your price for anyone, no matter the situation.

Using Time to Drive Value

Another great strategy to help sell at full price involves using the element of time. There is only one resource that is not replaceable and that is time. Use it to your advantage. When you communicate to the customer your price point, you must also state the specific time period that price is available. The shorter the time period, the better.

I introduce this issue last for one reason. If you do not think any of the other strategies I've shared in this chapter will work for you, then certainly the strategy of time is one that can work. Time is a wonderful tool to leverage against a customer's decision-making process. Yes, there are customers who will try to leverage time against the salesperson as a way to try to secure a lower price. Never let yourself make an offer to a customer without also including the date the offer expires. Whether you adhere to it is secondary to the point of putting a specific date in your written or verbal offer to the customer.

Time (particularly the shortness of time) always prompts a sense of urgency. When combined with your price point, time creates an additional reason to buy. Customers who believe they have all the time in the world to make a decision are more likely to engage you in more discussion when given a deadline. Sure, any additional discussion is a chance for you to learn critical information for closing the current sale and future sales, but it also can give the customer confidence to ask for a discount. Presenting your full-price offering in conjunction with a definitive date helps prevent the "delayed decision" syndrome. It also provides you with very succinct reasons to follow up with your customers, should they not make a decision to buy during your sales call.

Fully understanding how you can leverage time also allows you to structure packages differently depending on the customer. I'm not saying in a backhanded way that you should be negotiating with some customers by using different dates. What I'm saying is that knowing how to leverage time gives you flexibility to control your sales *without* entering into negotiations with any customers.

The ability to use your full price as a value-added tool is essential, and the more confident you are in your price point, the more you will be able to maximize your profit. If you don't care about the level of profit you and your company make, then feel free to discount at will. By the way, if you do adopt a strategy of discounting at will, be sure to contact me a year or two from now. I'll be anxious to hear how well the strategy is working for you—and whether you are looking for a new job. Yes, I'm being blunt, but there is no way you can discount your way to prosperity. Sorry, it just doesn't happen. You can discount your way to short-term survival. However, while you may be able to survive for a while, you really are only delaying the inevitable. A discount-at-will policy is not a business model that will ever survive. I refer to those who use it as "the walking dead." These are sales companies and salespeople who are only kidding themselves into believing they are successful, when in reality all they are doing is putting off the hard questions that need to be asked. Namely: What is the full-profit price point I need to be selling, and what is the strategy I need to be using?

CHAPTER 5

Prospecting That Works

ONCE, WHILE I WAS WALKING through an airport, I heard someone behind me calling my name. As I turned around, I recognized the other person as the president of a company I had done some work for a few years earlier. He asked me if I had a couple of minutes, because he wanted to talk to me about an issue involving his sales force. He said he always thought he had the best salespeople in the industry. His strong belief in the quality of his people was the reason he felt he never needed sales consulting services. I couldn't help but chuckle inside because just then, I knew immediately he was going to begin telling me about some problem with his salespeople and ask for my help in solving it.

I was right. He explained that he had come to realize that what he really had was a sales organization that was very good at answering the phone and managing existing accounts, but terrible at finding and selling to new customers. When he was finished talking, I shared with him my assessment: What he said was nothing new. Many companies experienced the same thing, and any company that had not experienced it yet eventually would. It's almost an unwritten rule of sales.

Past Growth Doesn't Guarantee Future Growth

The problem he was describing stemmed from the fact that his company had enjoyed several years of very good growth, and as a result, the sales force never had to truly go out and *sell*. In other words, his salespeople could easily coast along on the natural growth in their industry and the power of their advertising and marketing campaigns to bring in business. Now, because of changes within the industry, new competitors, and a host of other changes in the marketplace at large, his company found itself in the position of not only being unable to grow, but also losing business rapidly. Worse yet, the company didn't have a sales development pipeline to offset the loss of existing customers by replacing them with new ones.

At least the president of this company realized the issue he had. His difficult situation was not due to the pricing structure of his company's products and services. His problem was his sales force was not really a sales force at all, but rather a customer service team. (I sometimes have to be very blunt in how I share my opinions regarding sales, and this is one of those occasions.) Salespeople are supposed to find sales—

added sales and new sales, not sales that would have occurred whether they acted or not. I believe that companies should pay their salespeople very well, but not for sales that require them to do nothing more than answer the telephone or respond to an e-mail.

Finding New Customers Is Not an Optional Job Activity

Salespeople should be required to go out and find new customers daily. They need to attract customers not with a low price, but rather with the value proposition each salesperson must clearly demonstrate. When salespeople sell to new customers based solely on the merits of a price discount or some other attractive offer, in my book these salespeople are not really selling. They are merely taking an order. This book is about maximizing your profit. It starts with the very first sale. If you don't make your full profit margin on your first sale to a new customer, then what makes you think you'll be able to get it on the next sale?

The failure of salespeople to spend a proper amount of time prospecting and maintaining a strong list of sales prospects is typically the reason they also struggle with holding firm on pricing with existing customers. When salespeople believe the customer they are currently working with is the only customer they have, it creates intense pressure that almost always ends up clouding their decision-making abilities when it comes to closing the deal.

Prospect or Suspect? Do You Know the Difference?

Before we get deep into the subject of prospecting, let's get one thing settled right now. Not all prospects are real prospects. Sometimes a customer who may appear to be a prospect is nothing more than a "suspect." My definition of a prospect in the business-to-business environment is someone who has provided you with some piece of proprietary information that is not publicly known. Similarly, in the business-to-consumer environment, a prospect is someone who will share with you information that hasn't been shared with someone else. A prospect who believes in you as a salesperson will confide in you something of interest that is not known by others. The reason I use this definition is simple. Suspects will monopolize your time for the sole purpose of obtaining information from you that they can leverage with another salesperson to get a better deal. The most valuable resource you have as a salesperson is your own time. You need to guard it carefully, because when your time gets misused or wasted, the activity that tends to get pushed aside first is prospecting.

Is Prospecting Ingrained in Your Daily Routine?

Prospecting must be as routine as taking a shower. You have to do it on a daily basis. The rare occasions when you don't do it should be because of unusual circumstances. Prospecting must also entail actually *talking to prospects*. When they

are supposedly prospecting, all too many salespeople are
doing nothing more than shuffling paperwork or surfing the
Internet, all under the guise of getting ready to prospect.
Salespeople may try to justify themselves by saying they are
planning to prospect or gathering information to begin prospecting, but the truth ultimately cannot be hidden: *They
aren't actually contacting prospects.* I can't tell you the number
of times I've worked with companies, large and small, and
after we begin to break down the data, the glaring reality
surfaces—the salespeople have spent very little time actually
prospecting.

Can't Prospect? Then You Can't Sell

If you can't prospect, then you can't sell. Again, I am being
blunt, but salespeople will sometimes tell me that they are not
effective at prospecting, but in everything else associated with
selling, they are superstars. I'm not buying it. They may be
superstars in customer service, but definitely not in selling.
Selling is synonymous with prospecting. The two cannot exist
independently.

The best method for prospecting is by first establishing
daily, weekly, and monthly goals as to what you personally
are going to achieve from prospecting. It is absolutely essential
that you have distinct goals for prospecting. Otherwise, prospecting will get mixed in with everything else you do. If salespeople believe they can achieve their sales goals without
prospecting, they will almost always stop prospecting.

What Is a Prospect?

I stated previously that the definition of a prospect in the business-to-business arena is someone who will share with you some proprietary information—information that is not known publicly by people outside of the company. If you sell to consumers, then the definition is an individual willing to share with you a piece of information others would not know. With this definition of a prospect, I firmly believe your goal early in your meeting with the customer is to get the customer to reveal to you information that would fit this criteria. If customers are not willing to share this level of information, then they are only suspects. Once you've classified a person as a suspect, you need to be extremely cautious about any additional time you spend with that person.

New salespeople who are eager to prove their worth are quick to spend time with anyone who will listen to them. Whether you are a new or seasoned salesperson, if you want to be a high-profit salesperson, you need to spend time only with people who are motivated to buy from you. Now, I'm not advocating that whenever you are meeting with someone the first question out of your mouth should be, "Will you reveal to me your deepest, darkest secrets?" What I am advocating is that you have a series of questions ready that will get the customer moving in the direction of sharing proprietary information with you.

The reason I'm big on getting customers to reveal exclusive information to you is to prevent you from spending time with people who may show incredible interest in what you have to say, but only for the purpose of doing their own information gathering that has nothing to do with buying from you. For example, they may already know which vendor they are going to buy from, but before doing so, they are compelled to speak with at least three vendors. (You are just one of the token vendors in this scenario.) Or they may be gathering information from you so that they can use it as leverage to secure a better deal from another vendor. Finally, the worst type of offenders are customers who meet with you only to gain some general information to support their position to postpone making any decision at all at this time.

Let me confess that I have been guilty of being the suspect in all three of these scenarios. During my tenure working for several large corporations, I found myself gathering information from salespeople when I had no intention of buying. What's absolutely embarrassing to the sales profession, however, was how few salespeople actually caught on to what I was doing. They would continue to pester me for weeks and months after I had obtained from them the information I wanted. It's unfathomable the amount of time and money these salespeople spent not only on phone calls and correspondence, but also in travel—all in an attempt to have what they felt would be a crucial meeting with me. What a waste! That's why I'm such a strong advocate of monitoring how you spend your time prospecting. I want you to avoid spending your time with suspects.

Not All Prospects Are Created Equal

We've been talking about the value of a prospect and the cost of a suspect. Now let's add another layer to the discussion, because not all prospects are created equal. The best way to determine if a prospect is a *good* prospect is by asking the person to do something for you. I don't mean do something like wash your car. What I am talking about is asking the prospect to do something for you after the sales call is over.

That "something" could be to have your prospects send you some additional information, or review something you are going to send them. The basic idea here is that people who are truly interested in buying from you will participate in the buying process if they believe there is value and it will help them. Prospects who are merely collecting information to support their own agenda are not going to agree to do anything for you.

As with other methods for gauging your prospects, it is important to understand that this one is not universal. There will be times when a prospect with whom you are working is indeed a good prospect, but just isn't going to follow through and do the "something" you have requested. It may be because of the person's time constraints or some other reason. In general, though, I have found that a person who is willing to do something for you *after* the sales call is a motivated prospect.

Assumptive vs. Inquisitive

It may sound like a strategy an attorney might use in a courtroom, but I'm talking about the two primary approaches you can take when making a prospecting call: assumptive vs. inquisitive. The general rule is this: If it is a small company and

I am talking with the owner or principal player in the company, then I will use the inquisitive approach. If, on the other hand, I'm dealing with a large company, the only approach I will use is the assumptive method.

The primary difference between the two is in the type of questions you ask. If you are using the inquisitive approach, you ask open-ended questions centered on the potential customer's business. If you are using the assumptive approach, the questions you ask are more confirming in nature about the industry in which the prospect operates.

The Assumptive Approach

When I worked for a company with annual sales of $20 billion, the last thing I wanted to do was to spend time with vendors who were not comfortable dealing with big companies. I wanted to work only with vendors who understood how large companies worked and the pressures executives in a large company are under at all times. If a vendor walked into my office and made even the slightest comment about being "wowed" by the size of our company, I would immediately look to end the conversation. I didn't have time to educate the vendor and provide an orientation session. The vendor either understood how big companies worked or didn't, and those who didn't were gone. Simply put, I wanted to work with vendors who were similar to me and were comfortable dealing with big companies.

Vendors who were comfortable working with big companies would come into my office asking questions or making statements that demonstrated their knowledge of the industry and my company. The questions and statements showed they had done their homework. The salesperson's body language showed neither arrogance nor timidity, but rather comfort with the circumstances that are common within big companies. This is what I call the assumptive approach to prospecting. In summary, it is a process where you have done your homework on the company with which you are meeting and the industry in which it operates. You more than likely are already able to uncover some of the company's key needs.

Assumptive questions and statements are best built around current information available through research on the Web. The key is to understand the current issues facing the company you are about to meet. You should be able to either draw a conclusion on the issues and/or ask questions about the issues in a way that reveals you have an awareness of what the company is facing. Enter into an assumptive meeting with at least three questions each on four to five different topics or issues. That means you must have twelve to fifteen questions ready to go. I like having this many questions because it gives me enough backup material for continuing the discussion in the event additional people wind up joining the meeting. As an example, the meeting might begin with one person, and you have the opportunity to ask three questions on three topics or issues. You're feeling good about the way the sales call is going, and then the person with whom you are meeting invites you to meet with one or two additional people. Suddenly you have a new audience. By having prepared questions at the ready that you have not used yet, you can further reveal to everyone that you are more knowledgeable about their company than they had likely expected.

One last point about using the assumptive approach to prospecting: Do not ask your questions as if you were working from a checklist. Ask one question and allow the other person (or people) to respond. The responses you receive will help clarify for you if the issue you have brought up is relevant to them. Your goal is not to embarrass the prospect. You want to engage the prospect in a meaningful discussion and ask follow-up questions based on every comment the prospect shares. Use your follow-up questions as your guide to where the prospect wants to take the discussion. Early in the meeting, you should be listening for key issues the prospect brings up more than once. Anytime people bring up the same item more than once, it signals something is a concern to them and is worth exploring even more.

The Inquisitive Approach

The opposite of the assumptive approach is the inquisitive approach. The best way to explain this approach is by sharing with you a personal story. I was sitting in the office of a small manufacturing company in Asia. Because I knew nothing about the company, the only approach I could take was to allow my natural inquisitive nature to come through by asking the owner questions about his business. The more inquisitive my approach, the more engaged the owner became. The reason is simple—I was showing interest and allowing the owner to guide the discussion. Yes, I was playing to the owner's ego, but in so doing, I was able to get him to share with me an astounding level of information about his company.

People who have started their own companies are always eager to share their success story. They are always eager to let others know the details of their success, and there is no better way for you to develop a relationship with this kind of prospect than by letting the other person do all the talking.

Using the inquisitive approach is easier than the assumptive approach because it does not require the same level of preparation. The only ingredients necessary are your own sense of curiosity and your ability to carry on a conversation that is not centered on you. Additionally, it is important to always show interest and respect, regardless of what the customer is talking about. Often a key person in a small company will spend time talking about something you might see as not all that important. Although it might seem unimportant to you, it is important if the prospective customer is taking time to talk about it.

There is one challenge you should be aware of that can come up when you are making multiple sales calls on the same day that may require you to use the inquisitive approach with one prospect and the assumptive approach with the other. Mixing the two approaches can be fatal, especially if by accident you start using the inquisitive approach on a large customer. That mistake will dramatically reduce the likelihood of your success. So be sure you are fully engaged in using whichever approach is appropriate to the sales call on hand.

Tactical Comments and Questions: The Price Squeeze

Chapter 10 is devoted to the value of strategic and tactical questions when selling to the C-suite. For now, let me just say that strategic and tactical questions are also critical in the prospecting phase. Listen to how prospects respond to your questions and pay close attention to the questions they ask you.

People who are price-oriented usually ask more tactical questions. These questions are centered on specific issues, such as quantities, dates, and price. When customers focus their comments on tactical issues, you should not necessarily assume they are motivated buyers. What you *can* assume is that they are price buyers. Inexperienced salespeople will often seize upon the direction the customer is taking the conversation and they'll start trying to close the sale. If the salesperson is dealing with an experienced customer, there is no way the salesperson is going to win. The customer will push hard to gain as much of a price advantage as possible. My experience is that sometimes prospective customers of this type are motivated to buy, and on occasion they won't push on price. Rarely, though, will they ever become the high-profit account that you really desire.

Tactical questions do have a role in the prospecting phase, but early on they should be centered on topics that allow you to qualify the parameters of the prospect's expectations. An example of a tactical question might be something like, "Do you typically place your orders on the tenth of every month?" By asking a question like this, you will be able to begin qualifying how to serve the prospect should he become a customer. If you ask the customer a tactical question and he chooses not to answer, you should move immediately to asking strategic questions.

Strategic Questions Lead to Long-Term Relationships

Strategic questions are those that are going to allow you to develop a long-term relationship with the customer, and most likely a relationship that is profitable for both you and the customer.

Strategic questions involve topics where the answers are not always clear-cut. Often, strategic questions deal with things that may or may not occur in the future. An example of a good strategic question would be, "What do you think will be the big changes the industry is going to deal with next year?" The idea is to get the prospect talking *and* thinking. Salespeople who ask strategic questions are always going to be seen in a different light than the vast majority of salespeople who are only able to think in a tactical manner.

When you find prospects who want to discuss strategic issues, you immediately should plan to increase your focus on them. These are the types of prospects who have the ability to significantly enhance your bottom line. Customers who are strategically focused are those who are not overly concerned with the immediate cost of something, but rather are looking at the long-term benefit of what they are going to gain. As I mentioned at the outset in Chapter 1, customers don't *buy* anything—they only *invest*—so you can see the importance of understanding and providing the benefits these customers desire.

Aim High When Prospecting

The discussion of strategic and tactical questions underlines why it is so important to sell as high up in an organization as you can. A common saying is that the only person who is truly authorized to buy is the CEO. The higher up you are able to reach in an organization, the more strategic your questions and discussions need to be. If you are dealing with somebody high up in an organization and you are asking tactical questions, you run the risk of being viewed as somebody who is wasting the executive's time and should instead be talking to somebody much lower in the organization. Should this occur, your ability to maximize your profit is gone. You will be viewed as a supplier of commodities.

Make Prospecting Part of Your Daily Routine

The best way to prospect is to make it part of your daily routine. I recommend you make sure it's the first thing you do at the start of the day and immediately after lunch. By starting off both halves of your workday prospecting, you will significantly increase the amount of time you spend on it. The only caveat to this advice is that the worst time to prospect is Monday morning. Most people typically use Monday mornings to organize their workload for the week and to hold internal meetings. Trying to contact prospective customers on Mondays often will result in very short conversations, if they are even reachable.

Another approach can be to set aside half days to prospect during the week. An example would be Tuesday afternoon, Wednesday morning, and Thursday afternoon. The half-day approach can be an effective way to get into a groove with your prospecting activities. It also allows you enough time to make telephone calls, send correspondence, and make in-person sales calls. The downside to the half-day approach is that you have to be willing to put aside other things, such as dealing with customer issues that may arise during any given day. If you allow yourself to get distracted by customer issues, you will find that you rarely make the time to actually prospect. To help you deal with this issue, you need to be working in sync with your customer service department or other people in your company who can handle issues in which you do not have to be personally involved.

Holiday Prospecting

This may surprise some of you, but the best time of year to prospect is during holiday weeks, particularly the period between Christmas and New Year's. When I ask salespeople if they typically spend this time prospecting, they are quick to say "no." What this tells me is that they are more interested in their vacation time than their work. I'm not going to jump into the middle of this argument except to say this: Customers you gain during a holiday period tend to be more profitable than customers you attract during the regular part of the year. With that insight, what do you think you should be doing the week between Christmas and New Year's?

Prospecting during holiday periods—especially by telephone—is highly effective for several reasons:

> During the holidays, you will be able to reach people you normally can't reach.

> People are more willing to talk during holiday weeks than during other times of the year.

> Most companies are still conducting business during holiday weeks. In fact, your prospects may find themselves suddenly unable to get their current supplier to fill a request that you can then fill.

Reaching People You Can't Normally Reach

Because many people take vacation time during the holidays, it is not unusual for gatekeepers to be out of the office and away from their desks. This leaves the people you are trying to reach having to answer the phone themselves. It's a perfect situation. It's what you want. When you combine this situation with the fact that there are far fewer salespeople making prospecting calls during holiday weeks, you increase the odds of your call standing out.

Being More Relaxed Makes People More Willing to Talk

During the week between Christmas and New Year's, most companies experience a slow period. There are fewer people in the office, and the ones who are there tend to be in a friendly and relaxed mood. In other words, they are more willing to talk to nearly anyone! During this period, you'll find your discussions often reveal far more information than you would be able to uncover during a phone call at any other time of the year. A positive outcome of these phone calls is that serious buyers will remember you were the one who reached out to them during the holidays. They'll be impressed that you are not like most salespeople. Salespeople who are actively engaged in selling during the holidays are also the salespeople who care about following up with a customer. Isn't that what any customer wants?

Better Positioning Yourself to Become the Vendor of Choice

This point has to do with where your full margin can be made. If you can help a customer who is in a bind, you will always be able to achieve a higher profit. For any salesperson who is trying to secure new customers by essentially taking them away from a competitor, holiday prospecting is one of the best strategies you can use. I've seen many salespeople land a new customer during the holidays by calling prospects and being able to help the prospect with a "rush" order that their current vendor is not available to fill. That's because vendors who feel secure in their sales and believe their customers are loyal to them will either close during the holiday weeks or operate with a skeleton staff, creating an ideal opportunity for a competitor to fill the void. The level of service you provide the customer in helping now is going to earn you the right to serve the customer again.

Just Do It

Prospecting comes down to one thing—*you simply have to do it*. Failure to prospect is going to take profit out of your business. The loss of profit is due not only to your inability to bring in new customers, but also to the tendency to offer discounts to your current customers because you are afraid of losing them.

Do not allow yourself to fall for the myth that you can't prospect until you have a good system in place and a computer management system to track everything. Sure, these tools are helpful and can make a difference in the effectiveness of your prospecting. However, if you wait for these tools and start prospecting only after you have "everything in place," you'll never get started. You will get in the habit of always finding something else that needs to be added or needs to be fixed before you start.

Forget about trying to have everything in place and instead simply start prospecting! Set yourself daily, weekly, and monthly goals you know you can achieve. Don't make your early goals so big that you have little chance of hitting them. Set goals low enough to achieve and use the momentum of that success to build your confidence more each day, week, and month.

CHAPTER 6

Sell More by Talking Less

ARE YOU INTERESTED in making more money by closing the same number of sales, but at a higher price? I am guessing your answer to that question is a resounding "Yes!" If I then ask you how you plan to achieve this goal, you might give me some complex process that would result in the customer paying more. However, in reality, the answer is not some complex formula. It's rather easy, but it requires focus and discipline.

It comes down to two things. First, ask more questions. Second, listen to what the customer tells you. I can't begin to tell you the number of times I left money on the table early in my sales career by failing to do both. For some reason, as salespeople—and I put myself in that group—we believe we have all the answers. We therefore think that the only way to control the sales process is to dump all this extraordinary wisdom on the customer. If you can't relate, you're either not in sales or you are in a huge state of denial. We all do it. We don't ask enough questions and we fail to listen to what the customer is telling us.

In my work as a sales consultant, I have the opportunity to not only work with thousands of salespeople, but also to spend time with many professional buyers who devote their entire day to doing nothing more than trying to get the best price possible. My conversations with professional buyers are incredibly revealing. One of the questions I love to ask them is, "How much talking do you do as compared to the salesperson?" The answer in almost every case is that the salesperson does the majority of the talking. Now, this discovery reinforces a conclusion I've reached in my years of consulting: *The professional buyer who typically secures the lowest price is also the one who talks the least.* Although my research is strictly based on interviews and I have never had the opportunity to statistically verify the results, I am comfortable sharing my hypothesis here in this book.

How Professional Buyers Use Silence

If the buyer who talks the least is the one most likely to get the lowest price, doesn't it make sense for us as salespeople to focus our efforts on getting the customer to talk? Sure it does. But to do that, you have to be far better than the typical salesperson who asks the most elementary of questions—questions like, "How is your day going?" Most salespeople mistakenly think they are good at listening and engaging with the customer, when in reality they are doing nothing more than annoying the customer. If you can't do any better than that, then—forgive me for saying it—you don't deserve to be securing a high price. The only thing you are going to get is the most basic of repeat orders. Anyone in a customer service position is capable of doing *that*.

Let's discuss further this concept of getting the customer to talk and, more important, getting them to tell you what you want to hear. Your goal is to get customers to share with you the benefits they desire and the needs they have. It's that simple. It's your job to take the desired benefits and needs they share with you and get them to see the full magnitude of what those are worth. You have to build on the pain and the gain of each one. Unfortunately, most salespeople think they can make their case by doing all the talking themselves. Although they may occasionally close the sale this way, rarely will it be at a price that maximizes profit.

Give Control to the Customer

Priority must be placed on allowing your customers to guide the discussion by getting them to talk as much as possible. When I share this advice with some salespeople, I get an immediate pushback. They believe if the customer drives the discussion, then it's only natural that the conversation is going to wind up being about price and how big of a discount the customer is going to receive. Actually, I say it's just the opposite. By allowing the customer to guide the conversation, you'll be far more likely to maximize the price, but only if you truly know your business. You must be more prepared than the average salesperson is going into a sales call. If you are truly prepared, you can allow the customer to have every appearance of calling the shots while, in reality, you're still the one who is in control. The secret is to not only know what you are selling from a features-and-benefit standpoint, but also to know how to engage the customer. I tell salespeople that they need to spend as much advance preparation time thinking through the questions they want to ask the customer as they spend creating the presentation itself. Too many times salespeople don't prepare their questions until they are waiting in the lobby to see the customer.

How to Use Your Personality to Ask Questions

When working on the list of questions, it's important to understand a few things. For example, a question that may work for one person won't necessarily work for another person. Each person has a unique personality, body language, and voice pattern, and all of these factors can and will affect the quality of a question. I'm also a strong believer that there are questions a female salesperson can ask that a male salesperson would not be able to, and vice versa. For example, a female salesperson would probably be able to find out more details about a customer's manufacturing process without much prompting. On the other hand, a male salesperson might be able to get information out of a customer regarding the customer's personal reaction to a product. In both cases, the nature of the response also depends on numerous factors, of which gender is only one.

To help you understand what questions will work for you as a salesperson, I recommend you keep a record of all the questions you ask your customers for a one- or two-week period. This may seem like a futile exercise, but the payoff will come when you begin to make notes about which questions are getting you the best answers. Keep track of this information, and after a week or two, you'll begin to see how certain questions are better than others. As your notes take shape, you then can begin using the questions you like best with other customers to see if you get similarly good responses. You also can begin modifying questions by taking part of one question and adding it to another. By merely changing one word or the structure of a question, you can gain even better responses.

Questions That Work for You

Your objective is to develop a personal list of questions you feel comfortable asking. Remember, however, that you aren't restricted to asking your customers only questions from this list. The list is your guide. It's your starting point and your comfort zone. My suggestion is that you have on your list at least ten questions you are most comfortable with. The next step is to then take these ten questions and rewrite them in a different manner. The idea here is to turn your ten great questions into twenty great questions so that you have backstop material for yourself.

In any team sport, there are the players who start the game and there are the players who come into the game later. By having skilled players who can come in and relieve the starters, the team has a much better chance of winning the game. The same dynamic exists when you have a set of revised questions. You may think your questions as originally worded are great, but there will be times when they fall flat depending on how the customer responds. A set of alternate questions—even if they are simply revisions of the original questions, some of which you've already asked—will give you the confidence to continue engaging the customer in dialogue.

This brings up an issue that trips up many salespeople during a sales call. They walk in with a few questions they want to ask, they work their way through the list of questions, they reach the end, and then boom, they're off to the races taking the customer through their presentation.

How Much Time Do You Talk on a Sales Call?

Asking the customer questions is not something you do only at the *beginning* of the sales call. It is something you need to do throughout the entire sales call. A rule I use is to never talk for more than twenty seconds without asking the customer a question. Think about that for a moment. Twenty seconds. *Can you do it?* It's amazing how long the typical salesperson will talk before engaging the customer. Often I've had buyers tell me how they have sat through an entire sales presentation without ever having to say anything. By the way, *engaging the customer* means more than getting a head nod. Engaging the customer means getting them to talk and share their opinions, ideas, and thoughts.

Tactics Buyers Use to Speed Up the Sales Call

At various times in my corporate career, I've listened to salespeople pitch me on any number of different things. I had a favorite tactic for getting salespeople in and out of my office quickly. First, I would tell them immediately that I was not going to be able to give them as much time as scheduled. I wanted to get them to cut to the chase and the core reason they came to see me. Second, I had a clock directly behind where the salesperson would sit and I would time how long I could go without having to answer a question or say anything. And, almost always, the salesperson would fall right into the trap and wind up talking faster, cutting out the "how's the weather" questions, and actually cutting out all of the questions.

The end result in each case was that I got the information I wanted, but the salespeople had little to show for it. They never learned what benefits I desired, and they also didn't get any perspective as to what I was thinking. You can see clearly where these calls wound up. Because I was with a large corporation, they would play their follow-up games: The more I held back on making any decision, they assumed, the better the deal they would make. After all, because I was with a big company I would naturally be placing a big order—and any profit they lost on any discount they offered me would certainly be made up with a bigger order. That was the exact opposite of how I was thinking. Any buying decisions I was going to make had to be done with the full assumption that my company was receiving a return on its investment. Price was certainly a key criterion, but by no means was it the only one. Whatever I was planning on purchasing still had to fit my strategic goals and objectives.

Why Salespeople Fail

In each case, the salespeople should have taken the approach I am presenting in this book: *Slow down and engage the customer in a conversation.* The purchases I wound up *not making* at all are too many to list here. The reason I never placed an order with any of them is because the salespeople were never able to get me to express my needs and the benefits I wanted. If they had, they would have then been able to match up their offering with my needs and potentially close a deal with me.

Along with having great questions prepared in advance, salespeople must also know how to ask those questions and what to listen for when the customer responds. Customers are going to be speaking in their own language, and as salespeople, we simply won't be tuned into that same language. So, it's equally important to learn to listen well.

An Example of Not Listening

Here's a great example: A few years ago I was doing work for a pharmaceutical company. My job was to work with a cross section of the sales force to develop a set of best practices. One particular day, I was making the rounds with one salesperson, calling on doctors' offices and looking for an ever-elusive two minutes of face time with the doctor. At mid-morning we entered one office, proceeded to introduce ourselves at the front desk, and asked if the doctor was in and if we could see him. The person at the front desk greeted us with a serious expression and said, "Dr. _____ is not here; he's in the hospital." Without missing a beat, the salesperson I was with politely asked if the doctor would be back later that afternoon and if it would be okay for us to come back at that time. Again, the office employee looked at us with a somber look and said, "No, Dr. _____ had a stroke last night and his condition is not good."

Now, you can imagine the look on the salesperson's face at this point. After apologizing and offering condolences and our best wishes, we scooted out of the doctor's office as quickly as possible. Had the salesperson carefully listened to what the employee was saying and picked up the visual clues, she wouldn't have so quickly ignored vital information that the employee shared. First, the salesperson would have noticed the solemn facial expression. Now, I'll give the salesperson a pass on this one, because it's not always easy to read another person's body language. The second item, however, I will not be so lenient about, because the office employee clearly used the word *in* instead of *at*. Anyone in the medical field dealing with doctors knows they are "at" the hospital making their rounds, not "in" the hospital. That small word implies something completely different, and the inattentive salesperson completely missed it. Needless to say, it was an awkward moment.

Learn Your Customer's Language

Stop for a moment and ask yourself, "Do I understand the *language* my customer is speaking?" The best way to educate yourself is by asking a follow-up question. Regardless of what the customer has to say, always be prepared to ask a follow-up question. Not only will you gain vital information, you also will begin to learn the lingo of the customer's industry. In the example I just shared, the pharmaceutical salesperson did initially ask a follow-up question (with regard to whether the doctor would be available later). Unfortunately, it was the wrong way to follow up because she didn't catch on to the fact the doctor was "in" the hospital. In this particular circumstance, a more appropriate follow-up question obviously would have been, "Is he going to be all right?"

Don't think for a moment that it is easy to master the type of listening that distinguishes a superb salesperson from a mediocre one. You can bet, though, that it's going to take a lot longer to master if all you do is spend your time developing sales presentations. You would be wiser to spend a bulk of that time developing questions that you then actually use during your presentation time.

With customers always looking for a better deal, it's essential you understand the customer's needs and desired benefits. Remember, earlier in this chapter, I emphasized that you want your customers to talk as much as possible and to verbally tell you what they need and want. Your objective is to make sure you do not get sidetracked by either presuming what your customers want or by misunderstanding what they tell you. In either case, the process begins with taking whatever information customers share with you and asking them a follow-up question.

The Best Follow-Up Questions

The types of follow-up questions I like best are short questions. As I like to say, "Short questions will get you long answers, and long questions will get you short answers." The best short questions are these:

> *Why?*
>
> *How come?*
>
> *Could you explain more?*

These questions are easy to understand and will always win out over the complicated questions many salespeople love to ask.

Put the Pride Aside: It's Costing You Money

The reason I believe salespeople don't ask more follow-up questions is because of pride. They feel it's beneath them to ask the customer to explain something in more detail. Put the pride and ego aside. It's costing you money. In fact, it's costing you big money! Sometimes customers themselves aren't quite sure what they want, so asking them to elaborate on their requirements gets them thinking in greater depth about what they want and need. When they respond to your follow-up question, they will discover even more needs that they have. I can't begin to tell you how often I've seen it happen, both in sales calls I've led and on calls where I'm tagging along to observe other salespeople. You might say it's the follow-up question that allows you to really start uncovering the customer's needs. And at this point you can begin to sense, finally, that you can make a profit on the sale. I'm a very firm believer that deals that appear to be going nowhere fast can turn into very profitable sales once the customer begins to open up in response to follow-up questions.

Professional buyers who have shared with me their views on follow-up questions also confirm my belief that most salespeople don't know how to listen. Buyers' comments have revealed to me that it's rare for a salesperson to even ask a follow-up question, let alone a follow-up question that is completely open in nature. The vast majority of buyers have told me that the typical salesperson may come in and ask a few questions, but most of them seem to be very leading and manipulative in nature. Excuse me for saying this, but is it any wonder many buyers dislike most salespeople? Would you like to spend your time listening to people talk way too much and only solicit your opinion with questions to which they already know the answer? I don't think you would like it. Possibly you are beginning to understand why many salespeople get beat up so easily from buyers over price. It's simple—the typical salesperson is very predictable in his approach to the sales call.

Expand Your Question List

Earlier in this chapter, I advised developing a list of ten great questions you feel comfortable asking and that you feel are most likely to get you engaging responses. I even suggested that you expand these ten questions into twenty by rewriting them so that you will always have backup questions at your fingertips. You can now add to this list the follow-up questions you're comfortable asking. The more comfortable you are in asking them, the more likely you will be to use them.

Just one tip: Don't make every follow-up question the same—for example, don't just ask "Why?" Although you want to keep your questions simple, you must also have a variety of follow-up questions to keep the customer engaged. In fact, when you get good at this approach, you can ask one follow-up question after another and you'll be able to allow the customer to guide the meeting. An example of this might be, "Could you explain what you just said again?" After they respond you could then ask, "Where else have you seen that occur?" Or you might ask, "Very interesting insight; what are some other thoughts you have?" More important, the more you allow customers to talk, the more they'll share with you their specific needs and desired benefits. You'll know you're doing well with this approach when you are able to conduct the entire meeting and not even get into the presentation you brought along for the sales call.

Do You Respect Your Customer?

Your ability to ask follow-up questions is going to depend significantly on the level of respect you have for the customer and the level of interest the customer has in you. The more respect you show your customers for what they have to say, the more interest they will have in sharing with you. Someone who asks a question by first complimenting something the other person said is showing more respect than the person who bluntly challenges every comment. I have to go back to the male vs. female salesperson perspective once more. Each gender tends to ask questions differently, but I can't help but point out that women generally do a better job of showing interest. Additionally, because women generally come off as less threatening to the buyer, they will often be able to get more of a response out of the buyer with their follow-up questions. This is a key reason why, when determining what salesperson should handle a particular customer, it is important to understand who the buyer would be most willing to interact with, a male or female.

The Two-Second Pause

There is an old joke that the shortest span of measured time is the amount of time that passes between the traffic light turning green and the driver behind you honking the horn to get you to go. Honestly, I believe the shortest span of measured time is the length of time between when the customer stops talking and the salesperson begins talking. It's absolutely frightening how quickly many salespeople start talking as soon as the customer stops. How does the salesperson know the customer is not just taking a breath before continuing again? Now there's something to consider—pausing to breathe before continuing. Unfortunately, many salespeople just jump right in the minute there is a nanosecond of pause. To them, there is nothing scarier than a lull in the sales conversation.

Sales calls are not designed to see how many times the buyer can be cut off. Many buyers talk in very short sentences, and I believe it is because they have become accustomed to salespeople jumping right back in as soon as they have the chance. The solution is what I refer to as the "two-second pause." This means that when the customer is done talking, you wait two seconds before responding. Some readers may be thinking, "There's no way I can wait two seconds! The customer will walk away on me." Fine, if two seconds is too much, then try one second. Whatever you try, it's probably more response time than you're allowing now.

I encourage waiting two full seconds, because it usually prompts the customer to talk some more. Salespeople who have incorporated this technique have told me how many times the customer will hear the pause and start talking again. Wow, that's incredible—getting the customer to talk more without even asking a question. Even better, in many cases the information these customers share the second time will be much more valuable than what they shared with you the first time. The results you achieve will vary based on the circumstances, and what you achieve may be different than what someone else has achieved. It is up to you and your style, but certainly you can achieve better results than you would without trying this approach.

At the outset of this chapter, I shared my belief that professional buyers who talk the least are typically the ones who get the lowest price. With this in mind, it's now time to turn the equation around and make the *salesperson* who talks the least the one who is able to command the highest prices.

How much time do you spend talking on a typical sales call? When I ask salespeople this question, they inevitably underestimate how much they really talk. The average salesperson simply talks too much. Throughout this book you'll hear me addressing this issue, because I believe it is the single biggest reason salespeople leave so much profit on the table. When you make a conscious effort not to talk, you'll be amazed at your ability to focus and to see things more clearly because you're not filling your mind with what you want to say next. This means you can truly listen to what your customers are saying, which is the surest path to understanding what their needs are and the benefits they desire.

Close Too Fast and You Lose Profit

In sales, we are obsessed with what it is we are going to say next. We're obsessed with making sure the customer sees how smart we are and how much we know. Finally, we're obsessed with the belief that if we can close the sale quickly, not only will we get the sale, but we will also get it for the best price. In most cases, though, this rush-to-the-finish-line closing doesn't serve the salesperson well, because the results don't reflect what the salesperson thinks is going to happen. It's time to put away your ego and realize it's not a race to see how quickly you can close a sale. (Unless, of course, you are selling tickets for a flight that is leaving in ten minutes!) What is most important is how you close the sale so that you can maximize profit.

By allowing customers to explain, in depth, what they specifically need and want, you will have the greatest opportunity to tailor your offering. The tighter the fit, the higher the price the customer will pay; the looser the fit, the lower the price the customer will be willing to pay. I imagine by now that you are beginning to see why it is so important to let the customer do the talking. And, as I've emphasized already, to get customers to do the talking, you need to spend ample time developing the right questions.

Ultimately, it comes down to the questions you ask and the way you respond to what the customer says to you. Your questions must not be manipulative in nature, and they shouldn't be questions the customer will immediately sense you already know the answer to. Yes, there are times when these types of questions are helpful (such as when you are trying to get the customer to narrow the options he is considering), but in general, you need to ask questions where the customer will share information you do not already know. The best questions are those that simply get the customer talking. If you are prepared and know your products, you'll be able to handle whatever the customer shares with you.

The More the Customer Talks, the More You're Prepared for the Next Sale, Too

There is still one more critical aspect we want to recognize in this strategy of selling more by talking less. A truly profitable sale is not only one where you maximize the profit on the current sale, but also one where you can lay the groundwork for the next sale. This is still another reason why you want to engage the customer in conversation as much as possible.

Sure, customers will help you navigate the current sale, but they also will provide critical pieces of information you can use to start cultivating the next sale. It's this approach of being able to have each sale lay the groundwork for the next sale that allows still more profit to be made.

Part of the "profit" you gain with this perspective is your time. If you can end each sale with a few needs already spelled out by the customer, then you have essentially accelerated the sales cycle. You already have some of the information you need for the next sale. This is the payoff for taking the time early in the sales call to engage the customer and allow the customer to control the flow of the meeting. What is beautiful about this approach is that most of the time, once you get customers talking, they won't even realize how they're providing you with the information you need to start engaging them on the next purchase. If you are engaged in selling services, you already understand how effective this approach is for developing key accounts. However, for the vast majority of salespeople, this concept is new. It is why I can't emphasize enough the importance of recording every piece of information the customer shares with you. Each piece of information is worth something—either today or at a later date.

Keep Your Eye on the Prize

The challenge of talking less to sell more comes down to being comfortable with your communication style. It's your communication style, driven by your personality, that is going to allow you to ask the customer the questions you need to ask.

But it takes some time and effort to get comfortable with this approach. One way to push yourself to ask the customer more questions is by simply keeping score. That's right. Keep score! During all of your sales calls from now on, have a piece of paper on hand and simply put a checkmark next to each question you ask. Don't trust yourself to count in your head, because halfway through your sales call, you'll forget to count or forget the accumulated number. By keeping score of how many questions you ask, you can start setting a benchmark for yourself. Then, with each passing week, your goal is to increase the average number of questions you ask on each call by one. Increasing your average by one shouldn't be too tough. That's the beauty of it. It's an easily attainable goal and yet the prize is absolutely huge. Your ability to close the same number of sales but at a higher price is the prize, and it's there for the taking by just asking one more question.

CHAPTER 7

Skip the Sales Presentation

LATE IN THE AFTERNOON on a beautiful spring day, I found myself sitting in the lobby of a large global corporation waiting to meet with someone I hoped would become a major customer of ours. This sales call had been weeks in the making. It had taken considerable time and effort to secure an appointment with this particular individual, who had the potential to single-handedly make or break my sales career. In truth, it had not been all my work. Sitting with me was an associate who had worked with me each step of the way in trying to get this meeting and prepare for it. All of the effort to get this far only served to emphasize the importance of this call, not only for us, but also for everyone else in our company. You might say there was a significant amount of pressure on the two of us as we sat in the lobby.

Before we left our offices to fly to meet the customer, we spent countless hours perfecting our sales presentation. The presentation we would be delivering was based on similar presentations we had made with other customers. We tailored it to fit what we knew would be the key items this important customer would want to discuss. Sitting in the lobby, we discussed for the final time how the two of us would handle this late afternoon sales call. We decided my colleague would do the introductions and then set me up as the expert who would go through the sales presentation. We both felt good about the roles we would play and, more important, we were confident about what we would be able to get the customer to agree to in terms of the next steps.

When the time came for us to be walked down the long halls of this global giant's corporate headquarters to the office of the person we were meeting, we found ourselves engaged in small talk with the administrative assistant. She told us how busy and frenzied the day had been for everyone. Soon we were standing in the entrance to the office of the person we were scheduled to meet, and a glance at his desk quickly told us how hectic a day it had indeed been. The desk was covered with papers and numerous reports. Although he smiled and gave both of us a strong handshake, it was clear things were not going to go as planned.

Even before we could move toward the chairs, the executive motioned to us that we should step across the hall to a conference room. He was embarrassed by how his desk looked. As we walked across the hall and into the conference room, he explained that he had been in tedious planning meetings for the last several days and had fallen behind on all of his normal work. As we sat down, he mentioned how nice it was outside and how he was hoping to make it home at a decent hour. I suddenly realized that all of the preparation we had done to get ready for this call was about to go out the window. I knew that if I attempted to take him through our PowerPoint presentation or show him the slick, glossy sales materials we had in our bags, we'd never be able to do business with this customer.

Even while the customer was still talking about how he wanted to get home at a decent hour, I was reaching into my bag to take out my laptop. As quickly as I placed it on the conference room table, I pushed it away from both of us and said, "Let's not spend time going through the presentation we could show you. Rather, let's just spend a few minutes talking about your business."

My sudden, about-face actions brought a huge smile and a resounding "good" from the customer. He remarked on how much he hated PowerPoint and how especially at 4 p.m. on a nice spring afternoon, after sitting in meetings for several days, he was glad his final meeting of the day was not going to consist of another formal presentation. Suddenly I found myself connecting with a person we had been trying to reach for months. It appeared that by being able to forgo what we had planned, we now stood a real chance of breaking into this new account.

For the next thirty minutes, the three of us sat in the conference room discussing the state of the business. The topics we talked about were strategic in nature and engaging. Our dialogue allowed the customer to share his perspectives, while at the same time we were able to learn a tremendous amount of information about his company.

Several times during our discussion, my colleague and I were able to ask a question or make a comment to share with the customer the essence of what we were selling. During the entire sales call, I never turned on my computer. Not once did I take out any slick, glossy sales materials. We used only our notepads to write down profusely everything the customer was saying. In the end, we were able to reach an agreement with the customer as he referred us to the specific department that could and would buy from us. The company became a significant customer for us. I can't help but conclude that one reason for our success was the shift we made at the last moment in terms of what we chose not to present to the customer.

I also strongly feel that the primary reason our initial call with the customer went so well is precisely because we had spent the time preparing the presentation. This may sound strange, but if we had not spent so much time preparing the presentation, there's no way the call would have gone as well as it did, for one simple reason—we would not have been prepared. I'm a firm believer in preparing for sales calls. I think the lack of preparation for a sales call explains why many salespeople are not successful.

Why Preparation Is Essential

There's a belief out there, especially among veteran salespeople, that they don't have to prepare for a sales call because they know everything there is to know and they can just "wing it." Rookie salespeople often overtake veteran salespeople solely because of the rookies' willingness to prepare. The comparison I like to use comes from professional sports. Could you imagine a professional athlete never practicing? No, there is no way professional athletes would be able to have any type of long-term success without practicing. Now this does not mean they practice and then only perform in a scripted manner during a game. No, they allow their preparation and their experience to dictate how they respond to each situation as it occurs on the playing field. It is their ability to be flexible that allows them to be so good at their game.

Preparing a Sales Presentation Does Not Mean You Will Use It

Preparing a sales presentation is the same thing as practicing for a big game. Let me share a quote I use often: "The best sales presentation ever made is the sales presentation never given." I came up with that quote right after I made the sales call I told you about at the outset of this chapter. It was the experience of suddenly finding myself having to give a sales presentation in a manner I had not expected that caused me to come up with that quote. Top-performing salespeople are able to give a sales presentation without the customer even noticing that they are listening to a sales pitch. When I was in the conference room with the customer, talking strategically about his business and allowing him to share numerous pieces of critical information about the company, I was really selling.

While the customer was doing the talking, I was actually delivering my sales presentation. I was delivering what I had spent hours working on, but I was delivering it in an entirely different manner.

Do You Know Your Presentation or Do You Know Your Content?

There's no doubt we were able to be successful with this customer only because I knew my material so well. I was not married to my PowerPoint presentation. For too many salespeople, what they know well is the flow of their PowerPoint presentation, not their material. When I'm working with clients, I ask the salespeople how successful they'd be if they didn't have any sales materials with them when they made a sales call. The answers I get run the spectrum, but in the end they confirm one thing: The vast majority of salespeople don't know what they are selling and they lack the confidence to sell without their presentation materials. I'm not saying there's no place for sales materials. They *are* an essential part when you are explaining the technical aspects of what you are selling or when you are going through other service items. Too often, though, they don't serve a purpose at all other than to be a crutch.

The challenge each salesperson has is to be able to deliver a quality sales presentation without any sales tools. When you can do this and do it smoothly, then you will have the opportunity to start climbing to the level of being a top-performing salesperson. To start, you must be able to share with your customer, in short ten-second sound bites, what you are all about. More important, you have to have a steady stream of questions you can ask the customer, questions that flow naturally and confidently during the course of your conversation.

My intention with this chapter isn't to trash the use of sales materials or PowerPoint. Instead, I want to emphasize how important it is to know how to use those tools. But if you are using any type of sales materials or PowerPoint presentation and you have to *see* them to be able to talk confidently about your product or service, then you don't *know* your material. I like to use another sports analogy; in this case, the example of a baseball card collector. If you collect baseball cards and are proud of your collection, then you have a number of cards about which you know every detail without having to look at the actual cards. In fact, when you do pull out the card, you start passionately talking about the card and what it means to you. When you show the card to someone else and that person starts looking at it, you suddenly find yourself sharing additional information about the player that isn't even on the card. It may sound weird, but you should experience nearly the same thing with your sales materials. You should know them inside and out. You should know every detail about them. When you reach this level of knowledge and confidence, then you are finally ready to leave the sales materials in your car or your bag while you merely have a conversation with the customer.

Use your sales materials as reinforcement tools that allow customers to keep you in the forefront of their minds after you leave. In fact, consider skipping the PowerPoint presentation altogether so that instead, you can focus your energy on creating classy yet brief sales materials you can leave behind with the customer. Remember, of course, that anything you leave behind with the customer has the potential to wind up in the hands of a competitor. My advice: Only put into your sales materials information that you would put on your website. Leave out customer-specific information until you absolutely have to share it, especially if it involves anything regarding price. You want to protect yourself as long as possible, and disclosing pricing information too soon gives customers the opportunity to find other suppliers who could beat your price. Nothing will hurt your profit more than finding yourself in a bidding contest with your competitors.

What About Skipping the Presentation on the Phone?

So far this chapter has talked about the benefits of skipping the sales presentation during an in-person sales call, but the same advice applies to a telephone sales call. The more you know your information and the more you don't have to rely on a script, the greater your success rate will be with telephone sales calls. Forgoing the script on a telephone sales call is the same thing as forgoing PowerPoint during an in-person call. But you need to know your material inside and out and exhibit strong confidence when dialoguing with the customer.

Once you are able to deliver a sales presentation without any materials, you will find yourself with an increased level of confidence that will start coming across on every other sales call, regardless if you have sales materials on hand or not. Customers will recognize your ability to communicate confidently, which can only help build trust—and customers buy from salespeople they trust. Dialoguing with the customer in a casual manner doesn't mean that you allow the conversation to deteriorate to where you are not talking business. What it means is that you are comfortable allowing the conversation to go in whatever direction the customer wants to take it.

Always Respect Time

One important thing to remember is that whether you are presenting in person or on the phone, you must always respect the other person's time. If the meeting was scheduled for thirty minutes, then be prepared to wrap up with the customer after thirty minutes. If the conversation is going well, they'll make more time. If it's not going well, they'll end it. Either way, you want customers to see firsthand that you respect their time. By demonstrating that you respect the customer's time, you are also showing your level of professionalism, which will undoubtedly be expected to carry over if the person you are presenting to becomes a customer of yours. For salespeople dealing with people at the top of any organization, this standard of conduct is especially critical. The higher up in an organization people are, the more they value their time.

Developing Your Presentation

To prepare yourself to deliver a sales call without a presentation, you first must develop your presentation. You start by laying out the key points you want to communicate with the customer. Along with each key point, develop at least two to three questions you can ask to get the customer thinking about that key point and why it is important to him. The more you can use questions to create dialogue, the more successful you'll be in making sure the meeting doesn't come across as a formal presentation. Just be sure the questions—and your delivery—are not so structured and scripted that customers get the impression they are still hearing a presentation, just without the normal sales props. The best way to avoid this trap is by knowing your questions so fluently you can ask them in any order and be able to take whatever answer the customer gives you and then ask a follow-up question on the spot, based on what the customer just shared. Chapter 6, "Sell More by Talking Less," is meant to help you get comfortable in asking questions without your approach coming across as a presentation.

The second thing you need to prepare in advance are talking points that include facts you can recite comfortably from memory regarding the "big picture." These are comments that have to do with the customer's industry. They may include questions or facts about key trends or areas of interest regarding the customer's competitors. Again, the key is to be comfortable and relaxed in sharing this information. The idea is to start off your "non-presentation" by getting the customer talking about some of these subjects. Your ability to engage the customer in these topics early on is going to help you understand the customer's level of strategic thinking.

In my experience, typically only strategic thinkers appreciate and see value in a presentation that is more a discussion than presentation. Tactically oriented people or those who are highly sensitive to price tend to shy away from these types of presentations. Because your attempt on every sales call is to maximize your profit, it is only natural for you to steer yourself toward the people who see value in the strategic-oriented presentation. If your meeting can be informal in nature, you will come away with better strategic information and ultimately will close sales at a higher margin.

How Many Calls to Close a Sale?

The downside to using the non-presentation approach is that it usually requires a couple of calls to close a sale. If your business plan is based on being able to close a sale on one call, then you may not want to embrace this approach. I have found, though, in working with numerous companies, that they actually close most sales with two or more calls, even if they have the stated objective of closing the sale on the first call. This tells me that management may be setting a goal, but that doesn't mean the sales staff will achieve it. And I also see the danger in management putting too much pressure on the sales team to close sales in a single call, which means the sales team is more likely to discount prices in order to make the sale on the first call. This may translate into sales, but at lower profits.

I share these perspectives to encourage you to examine your own sales process. I realize some of you may be hesitant to abandon your sales call presentation for fear of lengthening the time it takes to close a sale. You may find, though, after implementing this approach, that it doesn't change or increase the number of sales calls it takes you to close a sale, but it does increase your bottom-line profit.

The final reason I'm a big proponent of skipping the formal sales presentation is that it allows you to be ready for whatever circumstances may arise. I'm continually surprised at the number of salespeople who wash out on a sales call solely because the customer suddenly changed the location of the meeting, or the length of the meeting, or the participants in the meeting. Many salespeople simply are not able to adapt to these changes because of how tied they are to their formal sales presentation. For some professional buyers, changing something about the meeting is standard operating procedure with salespeople on an initial presentation. Buyers will do this to merely catch the salesperson off guard, with the goal of learning quickly if the salesperson truly does know their business.

The ability to deliver a high-quality presentation without any sales tools is a mark of a salesperson who understands her business and knows how to communicate. Salespeople who are able to achieve this flexibility are more successful. In almost any situation they are able to discern where there is the chance to close a sale. They also are able to communicate on a deeper level with customers, allowing them to see opportunities that other salespeople would miss. In all cases, the end result is more profit for the salesperson and more satisfaction for the customer.

Leverage Knowledge to the Fullest

IF YOU WANT TO LOSE a sales negotiation fast, all you have to do is go into the negotiation without knowing anything about your customers, especially what they need and desire. Going into a negotiation without knowledge is like trying to drive an automobile without being able to see where you're going. Many salespeople think they can still be successful selling without being knowledgeable about the customer. These salespeople believe all they have to do is show the customer what they have to offer, and for some magical reason, the customer will buy.

Yes, the customer will buy if the price is cheap enough or the immediate need is great enough. But the problem with both of those situations is that the salesperson will leave a significant amount of money on the table. In the first case, the salesperson's profit is not maximized because the price has been discounted. In the second, the salesperson has not taken the time to learn all he can about the customer but is just glad to make the quick sale based on need.

The issue of not having enough knowledge of the customer to close a sale at the highest possible price is not the only problem here. Just as big a problem exists when salespeople don't have enough information to even know if the customer is worth spending time on.

From salespeople spending too much time with prospects that are nothing more than suspects to salespeople spending hours developing a detailed presentation on a product or service the customer clearly does not need, it all comes down to one thing—knowledge. Or I should say, the *lack of* knowledge.

The level of knowledge salespeople have about a customer will impact directly the amount of profit they will be able to maximize from the customer. As basic as this is, I am amazed at the number of times salespeople go into a sales call without having the knowledge they need. Worse yet, they come out of the sales call not knowing anything more about the customer's needs. No wonder there are so many salespeople struggling to make their numbers. They spend their time developing knowledge about what it is they are trying to sell rather than spending time gaining knowledge about the customer.

It starts with knowing the customer's exact needs. One of the first rules about negotiating is to never negotiate with anyone until you know that person's exact needs. The same is true in sales. If you don't know the customer's needs, you'll never be able to negotiate successfully. Unless you have knowledge about what the customer wants, there is no way you can even think about maximizing your profit.

The Customer Is Seeking Knowledge, Too

Before I go any further, let me say knowledge is also important from the customer's perspective. Your customers' ability to obtain knowledge provides them with leverage. Some people take this to mean that a knowledgeable customer is more likely to secure a better deal. Sometimes yes, but not always. I've seen situations where both the salesperson and the customer know a tremendous amount about each other, and not only is the salesperson able to maximize profit, the customer also is able to maximize benefits. In other words, a win-win situation! The days of keeping the customer in the dark are long gone. The Internet and the wealth of information at every customer's fingertips have more than diminished the idea that salespeople can be way ahead of customers with regard to information.

Leveraging Knowledge

It's not enough just to have knowledge; you have to have the right knowledge and then know what to do with it. We've probably all met an incredibly smart person whose IQ is clearly far above average, yet who at the same time is totally clueless when it comes to the basics in life. The expression "absentminded professor" aptly describes some people. In sales, our job is not to just acquire knowledge, but to know how to leverage it.

There is a reason I put this chapter on knowledge at this midpoint in the book, after we've already talked about how to get your customers talking by asking them questions and developing a technique to dialogue with them. My hope is that you won't fall victim to what I refer to as "false facts." This is where a salesperson hears the customer say something and, without even validating what the customer says, starts thinking it is some sort of secret-sauce recipe that will unlock millions of dollars of profit.

False Facts

Think back over your career and the times when you have gone after something based on a single piece of information. I'm embarrassed to say how many times I've done it. In fact, even after thirty years of selling, I still can fall prey to false facts on occasion. The reason is that salespeople tend to be optimistic—and I should add, salespeople *better* be optimistic, because if they're not, they most likely are not going to last long in sales. Being optimistic means we can be sucked into believing things a more pessimistic person would ignore. As a consequence, we are susceptible to chasing a false fact, not just at the beginning of our career but throughout our entire sales career.

Being knowledgeable comes down to making sure any information you get is good information and ultimately information you can use. I believe that every piece of information we can prove is true is valuable. (And, on occasion, even incorrect information can still be valuable.) We gain knowledge from a number of places, both from the customer and from outside sources. Your ability to apply this knowledge to a particular customer, both in preparing to sell and during the actual sales process, is what you should spend more time on.

Some salespeople don't give as much attention to customer information and knowledge as they should, and I believe it's because they don't have enough time to do everything. As a result, they end up devoting time to those activities that broadly apply to as many customers as possible and only spend time on matters that are specific to a particular customer if there is an obvious issue to address. I believe this tendency also explains why salespeople leave profits on the table. You will leave profits on the table when you fail to understand fully what the customer wants and needs. That's the information that proves valuable, but we have to get it from the customer, recognize it, and capture it. I'm a firm believer in double-checking each fact or piece of information you receive on any customer. You need to find two sources of information, either asking the customer to explain more or developing additional contacts within the customer's company. You have to be diligent in verifying information if you want to avoid being sidetracked by false facts.

How Do You Track Customer Information?

Let me take a moment to challenge you on your customer record-keeping. I continue to be astounded at the poor level of information most salespeople maintain on their customers. Sure, nearly every salesperson has recorded the critical information such as customer names and contact information. What tends to be missing are vital pieces of personal and professional information about buyers, their company, and their industry.

If you don't have a system in place to capture this information, then set one up right now. If you have a customer management system in place, ask yourself if you are using it the way you should. Be honest with yourself when you answer this question about the information you have on each customer: What piece of information is absolutely essential for creating a sale with this customer? If you don't have any information in your customer database you can identify as the key to securing a sale, then you are not using your system to the fullest extent.

The information you gather serves several purposes, including:

1. Giving you something you can use to follow up with the customer

2. Equipping you with material to validate or discredit another piece of information

3. Providing you with material you can use to support your proposal

4. Giving you glimpses into the customer's decision-making process

5. Furthering your ability to close the sale

6. Building a reservoir of information you can use on the next sale

7. Improving your ability to work with other customers

I've only listed seven, but I could have listed twenty-seven. My point is to help you see the importance of having as much knowledge as possible about your customer, the customer's industry, and the customer's competitors. Your level of customer knowledge is going to directly impact the level of profit you make on the customer.

Let's take a look at how you can maximize the first purpose: the ability to use information to follow up with the customer. The more your conversations with the customer can be about issues that are important to that customer, the more likely the customer will be to turn to you when he needs a solution. Each piece of information you gather about a customer gives you the opportunity to ask another question. If you are dealing with a company that is publicly traded, then each time the company releases its quarterly earnings or makes any other type of financial announcement, you should ask for your buyer's or contact's opinion. This may seem quite elementary, but in my conversations with many buyers, they say very few salespeople ask for their opinion. Obviously, if you become a salesperson who asks about key financial information, you'll stand out from other salespeople who are not asking these questions.

If you don't want to go the route of asking a question about your customer's quarterly earnings, you can simply use the released information to initiate discussions with other people in the company.

Visiting the Senior Officer

Years ago I was planning a sales call with a senior officer at a major company. Joining me on this call was my boss, who had flown into town because I felt having him on the call would help us get more information out of the customer and allow us to demonstrate the level of respect we had for the customer.

Over breakfast, my boss and I reviewed what we wanted to discuss, including the questions we were going to ask and our goals for the meeting. Knowing the company's quarterly earnings were due to be released, we checked the morning newspaper and, sure enough, there was an article in the business section detailing its earnings. Naturally, we made sure to mention this information in our discussion. When we entered the senior officer's office for the meeting, we immediately referenced the very positive earnings report and the nice coverage the company had received in the newspaper. The senior officer was, of course, appreciative and offered his perspective. We proceeded with our discussion. We concluded what we felt was a successful sales call and soon left the building.

Afterward, we realized we both had made a similar observation when we were talking about the newspaper article; we noticed the senior officer's body language change at that very instance. Neither of us knew the person well enough to know what his nonverbal signals were saying, but we both found it a little odd. After discussing the outcome of this sales call, we proceeded to visit a few more customers and forgot about the meeting we had already concluded.

Finally, at the end of the day while waiting in a restaurant to have dinner, I noticed a copy of that morning's newspaper and picked it up to briefly glance at it again. What I saw explained immediately the customer's reaction earlier that day. In our haste to get ready for the call and make sure we had what we thought was great information about the company's earnings, we failed to notice another article directly below the earnings report. The second article announced the promotion of the senior officer we had met that morning. *That* was the big news to him, and we missed it. Yes, the senior officer we met was proud of his company, but he was more proud of his promotion and the fact there was an article written about him in a major newspaper serving that entire area of the country. No wonder his body language changed. He was expecting us to compliment him and we didn't. There's no doubt he was shocked at our lack of knowledge, and he had every right to be. The lesson I learned from that experience is twofold. All information is personal and all information is important. Failing to see and acknowledge both of these lessons is done at great risk.

Using Information to Gather Opinions

Another way you can use information of this type—that is, publicly available information such as might be found on the company's website or from industry sources—is to ask other people in the company for their opinions and views. Doing so allows you to develop deeper relationships with contacts other than your buyer. I like this approach because it's not threatening to the buyer. It's true that some buyers are protective of what they do, and they do not like salespeople going around them to get things done. However, rarely will a buyer feel threatened by a salesperson asking other people in the company for their opinions on a topic as broad as the company's financials. The best ways to get these discussions going with other people in the company are simply calling them or sending them an e-mail. Certainly you would like to get some feedback from them, but even if they don't respond to your message, they still will have seen your name. Often this alone is enough to help deepen your involvement with the customer.

Validating Information

All information you receive needs to be validated regardless of its source. Anyone who has been in sales for any length of time can attest to the problem of receiving bad information. We all remember at least one sale we lost because we had bad information. This problem happens with both new and veteran salespeople. The only way to avoid having bad information is by being willing to validate each piece of information you come across. Again, this process of validating information creates great opportunities to ask more questions. Naturally, it's always best to validate information with people in the company, but of course that's not always possible. You have to develop other sources you can use in the industry, on the Internet, and elsewhere. The rule I use is that it's not information I can trust until I've received the same information from two different sources.

The more knowledge you have about a customer, the better. Don't ever forget, however, that information about the industry and your client's competitors is just as important. Many times buyers are so swamped with their own daily responsibilities that they do not have any time to do even the most basic reading about what's going on in their industry. This gives you a perfect opportunity to be their information source. I like to say that we as salespeople can be our customer's research and development department. It's our duty to help keep our customers informed. And, in order for our customers to be informed, we have to be informed. It requires time and effort on our part, but the payoff can be significant.

One of the most basic requirements, then, for you as a salesperson is to make sure you are linked to the trade associations your customers either belong to or should belong to. Additionally, it is essential to monitor any trade or industry news publications, something that has never been easier, thanks to the Internet and the power of search engines. Then, make it a point to share critical information you've acquired from these sources with your customers, as a way to demonstrate your commitment to them and their success.

The Power of Sharing Your Information

How you share information can take on a variety of forms. You can do it via e-mail, phone calls, or at the start of a sales call. It is best if you use all of the methods. Use e-mail and phone calls as a way to maintain correspondence with a customer in between calls. (We'll discuss this approach at greater length later in the book.) The third method is information sharing as part of the sales call, which allows you to get your customer's input on the subject firsthand. A quick test you can use is to listen for clues in how the customer responds to information you share or questions you ask. If the response is personal in nature, then you know the subject is important to the customer. If, on the other hand, the response is minimal or nonexistent, then you know the subject isn't of interest. Assessing your customer' interest level can then help you understand better what drives the customer's decision-making process. When customers respond to information you share with an engaging response, they care about the subject. This, then, becomes the perfect subject for you to use on your next sales call to initiate discussion.

The more you can tie your discussion and, in particular, the first part of any sales call to the critical issues the buyer is facing, the more engaged the customer is going to be throughout the entire call. This is why I believe the worst presentation any salesperson can make is what I'll refer to as the "capabilities presentation." It starts off with salespeople talking incessantly about how they have all the capabilities necessary to serve the needs of the customer, before even knowing what these needs might be. Recognize this type of presentation? At one time or another, we've all presented them, complete with the 100-page document full of absolutely nothing of interest to the buyer.

Knowledge Can Help Open the Next Sale

Knowledge has value, not only when it comes to the immediate selling opportunity but also when setting up the next sale—which is why I'm a big proponent of always recording every piece of information, regardless of whether you think it has immediate value. Each sale you make must lead to the next sale. Otherwise, you'll always be chasing new customers. When you can leverage knowledge to help open the next selling opportunity, it allows you to strengthen the relationships you've already built. More important, it allows you to leverage the customer's price/value expectations. Remember, you can never afford to discount your price. If you are going to build your business based on being able to sell to the same customers repeatedly, you cannot afford any type of a discount, as it will forever change the price/value relationship you've created in the customer's mind.

Knowledge vs. Information

Throughout this chapter I've been using two words interchangeably—*knowledge* and *information*. At this point I need to start splitting them apart to allow you to see why knowledge is more important than information. In sales, you have access to an abundance of information. There is no limit to the amount of information you can gather on just about anything. With the proper questioning techniques, there also is no limit to the amount of information from the customer you can gather that is not known publicly, whether it is business or personal information, or both. The challenge, however, is in knowing what to do with the information. That's when information turns into knowledge.

Buyers like information, but they like knowledge even more, and they will pay dearly for it. When I say *knowledge*, I mean information that has insight and has been interpreted to mean something of significance. Too many salespeople believe if they simply bring their buyers a lot of information, they'll be well received and their buyer will like them. As I said earlier, buyers may very well appreciate the information, but it won't allow you to be seen as a real sales leader. To achieve that status, you must be able to turn the information into knowledge the customer can appreciate.

Your Competitor May Have the Same Information

Keep in mind that if you are giving your buyer information, your competitors could very well be giving the buyer the exact same information or, worse yet, they could be giving the buyer the same information but with their knowledge added to it. When that happens, you'll be moved down the food chain in the eyes of your buyer. Your competitors will now be seen in a better light, making everything else they share with the buyer that much more important. Whenever you share any information with a customer, you must add your insights to the information. This allows you to demonstrate to the customer your knowledge and thought process. As a practice, sharing insights is especially critical for those salespeople who manage key accounts, where they deal with the same buyers on a regular basis.

Adding your insights is more than merely adding your perspective. It's about adding your *strategic* insights. When I say strategic insights, I'm referring to being able to take information and understand and explain how it may impact something one to three years down the road, or how it may impact a key issue the customer is currently facing. Adding insights of this type allows customers to see you as a thought leader who is looking out for them in a time frame that goes beyond the immediate sale.

To contribute strategic insights to information, you have to be able to see the full picture, which means you have to be diligent in your information-gathering process. Nothing will destroy a salesperson's credibility faster than professing to have strategic insights on a piece of information that turns out to be incorrect. Each time you share knowledge with customers, keep in mind that customers are drawing two conclusions. The first is what they think of what you just said and what they should say in response. The second conclusion is what they think of you and your credibility. The first assessment is certainly important, as it will give you a perspective on the customer's own thought process, which may help you close the immediate sale. However, for you to reach the top of the food chain and be in a position to maximize profit, it's the second assessment that is more important.

Your Knowledge Helps Create Trust

The more customers can see you as a person who is bringing them knowledge—facts you've interpreted for them—the more they'll place added trust in you. As your customers' trust in you increases, so too will the level of information they share with you. It is at this point where continuous exchange of knowledge between you and the customer becomes possible. Over the years, I've never found customers to willingly share strategic insights with a salesperson until they've developed a level of confidence in that salesperson. This confidence entails trust and integrity, and the customer seeing that you have the ability to think strategically.

Bringing knowledge to the customer does have limits. For one, salespeople who continually bring knowledge to the customer but fail to build a dialogue around it will soon find they don't have a customer to call upon. Again, you must do more than simply bring raw facts to the customer; you must take the time and effort to evaluate the information you are going to share and help the customer understand why and how this knowledge will benefit the customer's business.

Then there are some customers who do not value knowledge from anyone other than people within their own company. If you have a customer of this type, you still need to gather as much information as possible. However, the knowledge and insight you add will most likely stay with you.

Customers of this type tend to be short-term thinkers who are focused on merely dealing with today. These customers tend not to place value on anything other than the narrow perspective they have about what they are looking to buy. I'm raising this issue because I want you to recognize that this type of customer is not someone you want to try to build a business around. If you find customers do not place value in the knowledge you are bringing them, you can take that as a very good indicator they will be overly focused on price. These customers will exhibit very little loyalty to suppliers they buy from and, as such, are not where you want to be investing your time.

Young eager sales professionals often feel they turn this price-focused customer into a value-added customer. In nearly every situation, I've seen the young eager salesperson wind up learning the hard way that it's next to impossible to turn around a customer of this type.

Your Knowledge Can Create a Long-Term Relationship

The impact of your bringing knowledge to a customer is huge. It's the difference between merely making a sale and truly earning profit. I've seen many situations where a customer will continue doing business with a particular vendor based solely on the value of the information the salesperson brings to the buyer on a regular basis. When this occurs, the salesperson moves up the food chain to being somebody of definite importance to the customer. The measurement of success that I look for is if the buyer calls the salesperson and asks questions about the business or the industry at large that have nothing to do with whatever product or service the salesperson sells. When you receive these types of calls, where your customer is seeking your trusted opinion, then you have clearly reached the level of value to the customer where incremental profit is going to be made. You will make incremental dollar profit at the same time the customer wins by receiving incremental knowledge and insights that help the customer run a better business. Both the customer and you win by being able to leverage knowledge.

Sell More Without Even Being There

WE'VE ALL DREAMED of the perfect sale, the one where we no sooner walk into the buyers' office than they hand us a signed purchase order for the largest quantity we've ever seen. What's even better is that the buyers proceed to tell us the price they are going to pay is 5 percent more than the list price and the funds will be deposited tomorrow. *That* would be a dream, wouldn't it? I'd even call it an impossibly good dream. Your challenge is finding a way to make this dream come more or less true. It all starts with preparing customers for the sale and, more important, helping them begin to see you as a partner, rather than simply a vendor.

What makes this more of a challenge than ever is how

the Internet and the availability of information continue to change and influence how people sell and buy. Before the Internet, salespeople truly held the power. They had the information and the market research. Today, information is readily available to everyone via the Web or any number of other sources, which allows the buyer to be as knowledgeable as the salesperson. Buyers are now in a position to determine which salespeople they want to meet. As a consequence, salespeople must know how to leverage information (see Chapter 8) and the tools buyers use to determine if they want to meet with a particular salesperson or vendor. That's what this chapter is all about. I call it selling more without even being there, which is the concept of being able to create a level of awareness and confidence with the customer even before the actual selling process begins.

China and the Sales Catalog

In my work as a consultant, I've had the opportunity to work with companies in countries all over the world. On one particular occasion, while I was delivering a sales program in China, one of the participants invited me to visit his company. He was proud of his company and its products and he wanted to show off his operations to a Westerner. He also wanted me to meet with his sales department and share with them some of the things I had talked about during my conference program.

The business owner was extremely proud of how quickly his company had grown and acquired customers all over the world. His company manufactured items for construction and manufacturing industries. Upon entering his office, he immediately began telling me about the high level of quality they put into everything they made. At the same time, he laid in front of me several catalogs detailing what the company made. He handed me the catalogs as if he was about to unveil a lost Picasso painting. His voice and body language gave me the impression that my life would never be the same again. He slowly opened one catalog, showing me a page of pictures of his products. There were six pictures to a page, each in color, each with a short description of the size, dimensions, and other descriptive details of the item. At this point I felt he was forgetting to breathe, because I could see his chest heaving. I knew my only response was to compliment him on the catalog so that maybe he would start breathing again. I also knew I had to tell him that what he thought was the greatest sales tool ever was nothing more than the most basic industrial supply house catalog. It wasn't even worth the paper on which it was printed.

To this business owner, the catalog was the ultimate in selling tools. To a buyer, though, it was a piece of paper. He felt the catalogs his salespeople distributed to customers and prospects around the world were the reason for their success. He believed the catalogs reflected the same high level of quality as every product his company manufactured. Nothing could have been further from the truth. His success was not due to his sale catalogs or even his sales force. It was solely because of his low price. I share this story because it glaringly shows the problem we all have, whatever we may sell and wherever we may be located. We tend to be far more impressed with our sales tools than our customers are. It also shows that what we believe is helping us to be more efficient actually may be holding us back.

Too many times as salespeople, we are the last to realize what isn't working. We have a tendency to believe what worked in the past will continue to work in the future. This shortsightedness becomes significant not only when we are looking to close a sale, but also when trying to maximize the process. The first thing we have to keep in the forefront of our mind is the simple fact that customers have more information available to them than ever before. Chapter 8 talked about the need to turn information into knowledge in order to set ourselves apart from other salespeople. Now it's time to talk about how customers use information to decide if they even want to meet with us. In traditional business, we would refer to the process of putting our name and what we offer in front of our customers as "marketing." I like to refer to it as "vendor validation," which is basically the process prospects and customers go through to determine if they want to do business with us.

How the B2B Selling Process Has Changed

At the turn of this century, the business community was trying to figure out how to use the Internet and whether it had much of a role in the business-to-business (B2B) selling process. Well, we are way past that point now. Even so, still to this day, many salespeople do not comprehend the extent to which customers use the Internet to validate if they want to do business with a particular company or salesperson. I've had to pull more than a few salespeople aside at various companies and show them what online communities are saying about them personally. I'm not going to go deeply into this subject. But if you expect to make your living selling to others and being part of the business community in any manner, you had better be checking the Internet regularly to see what comes up when you search your name.

Putting Your Information Online

At the minimum, it is imperative for every salesperson to have a Google profile, a LinkedIn account, and a Jigsaw.com profile. You should also make sure your information appears correctly on your respective industry sites, especially any websites controlled by industry associations. Failure to be listed correctly on these sites is a huge mistake that many salespeople make. Many companies looking to do business with a new vendor or salesperson will use this type of information to ensure that the vendor or its representative is someone they want to meet. Sure, there are dozens of other websites and social media groups on which you can register, but from a business perspective, I believe these three—Google profile, LinkedIn, and Jigsaw.com—are "must haves."

Google Profile

If you are not familiar with what a Google profile is, think of it as the front door of your home on the Internet. Google, as the predominant search engine, naturally gives Google profiles their proper due in any search involving that person's name. You may think your name is unique, but with more than three billion people in the world, you can't even begin to imagine how many others may have your same name or a quite similar one. The sooner you get your profile added, the more likely you'll be able to control the use of your name.

To create a Google profile, go to https://profiles.google .com/ and follow the prompts. It really is quite simple.

LinkedIn Profile

You can create a LinkedIn profile by visiting www.linkedin .com and following the step-by-step instructions. One piece of advice—make sure you have a picture of yourself on your LinkedIn profile. When you don't have a picture on your profile, you are telling the world that you are not really serious about having your profile on LinkedIn. If you are going to be on this site, then fill out your profile completely. Of course, there is no need to make available your personal information, but certainly your professional work experiences and educational degrees are a must.

As long as you are completing your LinkedIn profile, take a couple of minutes and join LinkedIn groups that align with your industry and what you sell. It's an excellent way to not only prospect for new clients, but also to reconnect with people with whom you may have lost touch over the years.

Personally, I strongly advocate using LinkedIn as a B2B tool. Currently, there is no other website that comes close to offering the professional salesperson as many opportunities to network and raise his or her profile.

Jigsaw.com

Jigsaw.com is nothing more than the world's largest collection of business cards. That does not mean it's a worthless collection. In fact, it's a very powerful collection. Jigsaw.com is a database that consists of information that other people contribute in order to be able to earn points that allow them to look up other information. Your information may already be on it. If it is, make sure it's correct, and if it's not, fix it. You can visit the site at www.jigsaw.com.

Getting the Right Information on the Internet

Some people are nervous about being "found" on the Web, but the reality is that you will be found regardless of what you do. It is just the nature of how information is collected electronically. You may as well do whatever you can to make sure the information appears correctly. The days of being able to "hide" or remain completely anonymous are gone. You may be thinking, however, that there's no need to go to the effort of verifying your information because you sell for a major company and your customers already know you through your connection with your company. You are correct to a degree, but if you expect to be able to maximize customer profit and your own earnings, you had better make sure you are positioned the best you can be.

If you still doubt the merits of putting your information online, let me ask you a question. Would you show up for a sales call barefoot and wearing an old college T-shirt and expect to make an impact? Yes, you would make an impact, but certainly not a professional one. This analogy should help you start to see that your Internet profile is part of how you "dress" to meet a customer.

"Vendor Validation"

If you sell professional services or anything other than the most basic of commodity items, you need to realize that companies will often follow a person or another company on the Internet for an extended period of time before contacting them. This is why I call it the "vendor validation" process. The beauty of this process is that when you establish the right presence for yourself and your company on the Internet and a potential prospect who has done vendor validation calls you, that prospect is already a motivated buyer. This is the ultimate prize, because motivated buyers have a need and they are looking to you to help them.

I often say that "a customer who calls you is a full-profit customer." When someone has already completed the process of finding out if he wants to do business with you, the only thing left for you to do is to close the sale. By researching you and your company on the Internet and then choosing to call you, the customer has simultaneously decided *not* to call your competitor. What could be more beautiful than that?

As I've already mentioned, a prospect may follow you and your company for months or even years on the Internet before contacting you. It's important that your personal information on the Web is accurate, but I would add the same is true for your corporate information. Make sure your company's website is as good or better than the website of your number one competitor. Your corporate online presence is significant because when a buyer is selecting a vendor, the buyer will want and appreciate ways to defend his decision to superiors. If your company website is well maintained and managed and all the information it contains is current, it will validate your company's credibility in the eyes of the buyer. If your company's website is not current and laid out in a professional manner then your website is no different than the example I used earlier in the chapter about walking into a customer meeting barefoot and wearing a T-shirt.

Buyers may have to defend their decision not only at buying time, but also months down the road. It's known as "the IBM principle," which essentially says no buyer would ever get fired for selecting IBM, even if the company ends up paying a much higher price for the services. The point here is that a company will accept paying more for IBM services because of the confidence the name inspires. So, if you are looking for the answer to the magic question about how to command a higher price, we just found it: Create an image equal to IBM's. Anytime you present your corporate information, online or off-line, creating a high-quality image should be your goal, because even though there will be some customers along the way who won't want to do business with you, there definitely will be others that will. High-profit selling is not about doing business with everybody; it's about doing business with those customers who have needs and opportunities that align with your business model, and you want to win the confidence of those customers.

I use the example of IBM out of my real respect for the company and the premium reputation IBM has been able to develop. A salesperson or a company can't go wrong if they model themselves after IBM. If you choose not to model yourself after IBM, then identify another company, potentially an industry leader, to gain ideas you can use. Patterning how you position yourself by following other leaders will help you craft an image other people will look at with respect.

Becoming a Thought Leader

Being perceived as a leader in your industry requires you to do more than just have your profile information on the Web. You also have to make your thought process known. It is important to participate in discussion boards found online in the form of blogs or industry news sites. Every industry has several key sites where people from that industry share their comments and views. If you are an expert on certain subjects, taking a few minutes each week to add comments on those subjects will help bolster your image. Adding your commentary is a way for your current customers and prospects to get a glimpse into your thinking. Additionally, your comments will be picked up by search engines, allowing your name to appear in organic searches for keywords or phrases around those industry subjects and, over time, allowing you to be seen as a thought leader as your name moves higher in search engine rankings.

As I've already said, be sure you are paying attention to websites that are focused on your industry. Nonprofit trade associations manage many of these sites, and nearly all include discussion boards and blogs covering key industry issues. Take the time necessary to write high-quality responses to questions and blog posts. Don't think you need comment on anything but those topics that strike you as being important.

Writing Articles for Websites

Some sites even allow you to submit longer-form articles for publication. It is vital that your intent is to authentically share valuable information. If it sounds like you are making a sales pitch, the people who read these sites and run them will assume you are just trying to advertise. You'll lose credibility faster than Google can complete a keyword search. Your objective is to contribute meaningful insights, advance your industry, and allow others to see you as a person they can respect as an industry expert. In the process, you are also creating awareness for yourself, because when you contribute to industry-recognized sites, your industry peers will notice you.

Raising Your Profile in Trade Associations

If you are going to belong to a trade association, you might as well help lead it. There's no sense in merely being a member. You are either all in or not in at all. Volunteer to help with association activities. Yes, it takes time, but you'll create valuable relationships that will help further your presence in the industry. Not only will you build your presence, but along the way you also will learn a tremendous amount of additional information about your industry to help you with your selling process. I've never met anyone who has been a key player in an industry trade association who has not gained some long-term value out of it. The long-term value more often than not shows up as higher profit from both existing and new customers.

Time Well Spent

Selling more without even being there is more than just an idea. I know it works and, more important, it allows you to sell more and to do so at a higher profit. The sad part is that too many salespeople do not take the time to raise their professional profile online. Salespeople often lament that they are already buried by other work. But I tell them that if they don't take the time to create an online image for themselves and their company, they'll end up having less time to sell in the months and years to come.

Early in my sales career, I called on grocery stores. One thing my sales manager always told me to do was to make sure my products had signs on them. My sales manager knew that by having signs on the store shelves, customers would be more likely to buy our brands. More important, the signs were still selling for me long after I left the store. Yes, putting up the signs took more time, but in the end, it helped me sell more product.

The same thing applies to the Web. What you do on the Web stays on the Web. Each activity builds on the previous activity. So, take the time to put your information online. Also make the work effort of contributing thought leadership online, so prospects and customers will want to do business with you. It will pay off in more profitable sales in the months ahead.

10

Selling to the C-Suite

HIGH-PROFIT SELLING means finding ways to increase the profit potential of each customer or prospect. One surefire way to sell at a higher level of profit is by selling to those who bring a distinctive view to prices and margins. These people tend to occupy the C-suite and carry titles like CEO, COO, president, and vice president. They are the leaders of the company—the ones who look at things strategically first and tactically second. When customers view things strategically, they are much more concerned about the end result and the big picture of what the end result can create.

Understanding how C-suite occupants think is the first step in developing a strategy to sell to them. The problem many salespeople have is that they can get excited to meet with the occupants of the C-suite, but they don't know how to adequately prepare for the meeting. More important, they do not know the key things the C-suite executives want when meeting with people from outside of their company. When you understand the process and are able to develop a plan, you will be in a position to use the C-suite to not just close more sales, but to do so at a higher margin

What Language Do They Speak?

Imagine you show up for a sales presentation speaking English and discover that your potential customer speaks only French (and the extent of the French you know is "bonjour"). It is crazy to expect much success would come out of such a meeting, and yet this is exactly what happens when many salespeople try to communicate with somebody from the C-suite. The salesperson and the executive are not speaking the same language.

As uncomfortable as this scenario may seem to you, the salesperson, it can be equally uncomfortable for the other person, regardless of the person's title of CEO, COO, or senior vice president. If you are going to develop a relationship with anyone, you better know how to communicate with that person.

When dealing with the C-suite or, for that matter, any high-level person at a large corporation, you need to first understand where the executive is coming from. Yes, executives are human beings just like you and me, and yes, they have physical and emotional needs just like everyone else. Beyond that, the similarities begin to diminish. Senior-level people are driven by a different set of norms and expectations than other people in the company. The way they value time and information, and their ability to leverage both of them, is what allows them to occupy the C-suite.

When dealing with the C-suite, you need to take several things into account. Executives are really quite isolated, despite all the attention that may appear to be directed toward them. Their isolation reflects the fact that they are in a very competitive environment, and as such, they don't have the luxury of being as open with their thoughts and comments. C-suite people don't have multiple peers in the same company with whom they can talk or compare ideas. The people they frequently interact with are generally lower in the company hierarchy. Understandably, employees who may be several layers below the executives are going to exercise a lot of caution when talking with the C-suite level.

Because of their isolation within the company, C-suite executives are often driven to have relationships with people outside their company. However, in looking for people with whom they can connect outside the company, they are still going to be very guarded until trust is established. In fact, one way to connect with those in the C-suite is to build relationships with people who *do* have relationships with them. Executives associate with other executives and/or with people who, even if they are not part of the C-suite, still command that level of respect and trust. They may be peers of the C-suite crowd. If you expect to sell to the C-suite, this is the crowd you want to be a part of.

You may need to alter your activities to allow yourself to travel in the right circles. As an example, look at how salespeople connect with decision makers at Wal-Mart. In the 1990s, many manufacturers decided the best way to sell to Wal-Mart would be to have their salespeople and support teams located near Wal-Mart's offices in Bentonville, Arkansas. Obviously, this relocation strategy minimized travel expenses for the vendor's sales team, but more important, it allowed salespeople to travel in the same circles the Wal-Mart decision makers frequented.

One of the key values to which Wal-Mart has always adhered is that its employees are not influenced in any way by a vendor. This means vendors are not able to use many of the typical approaches of entertainment and incentives to develop a relationship with a customer. With the normal approach blocked, vendors wanting to sell to Wal-Mart found they had to get creative in interacting with Wal-Mart executives. So, they became active in areas outside of work situations, such as school and athletic activities where their children played alongside the children of Wal-Mart executives. They also became involved in community functions as well as church and synagogue activities. By traveling in the same circle as the people they were trying to reach, opportunities to connect naturally developed. This is the same approach you should use when looking to connect with the C-suite.

You may say this approach is not realistic for you, because there are either too many C-suite people with whom you are trying to connect or geographic boundaries limit your ability to enter into their circle of activities. There are still other ways to break through, and they start with being seen as a peer.

Attributes Needed to Connect with the C-Suite

Let's break down what it takes to be seen as a peer by people in the C-suite. It requires the following attributes:

- ► Trust
- ► Knowledge
- ► Respect
- ► Integrity
- ► Confidence
- ► Personal Control
- ► Value of Time
- ► Strategic Perspective
- ► Value of Assets

Some of these attributes are very basic and some are far more complex. Let's look at each one, starting with the bottom and working our way up, because the attributes at the bottom of the list are sometimes not as easily understood.

Value of Assets

This means understanding how assets can be used to one's advantage. The most basic asset is money, but assets also include numerous other things a particular company may deem critical to its success. Examples may be commodities such as oil, gas, or wheat. They also may include intellectual assets, such as patents, proprietary knowledge, and protective agreements. Whatever they are, they are important to those in the C-suite, and anyone who is going to communicate with C-suite executives must know what assets they value. It's not just important to know the assets, but also to understand how they are leveraged, how they are used, and the role they play in the company you're looking to associate with.

Strategic Perspective

People lower down in an organization are always going to be tactically focused. They are concerned about accomplishing things now, so they tend to be driven more by short-term goals. The further up you go in an organization, the more strategic people become. People at the top are usually the most strategic people in the company. This does not mean they're not concerned with immediate performance, but rather they have a better grasp on how short-term performance fits into long-term objectives.

One of the main examples is the strategic perspective on how to spend money. People at the top will spend money regardless of whether it is in the budget, provided they believe it will help them achieve an objective or allow them to position their company better strategically. This is the underlying reason why the best way to sell into an organization is to start at the top, because top-level executives are always less price focused than people lower down in an organization.

Value of Time

This may sound simple, but to executives in the C-suite, the value of time takes on an entirely new meaning. Not only is there the value of their time, but also the value of time on their assets. You might say that time has a compounding value. The more effectively time is used early on in the day, the more time is available later in the day. Furthermore, the more effectively someone uses time early in a project, the more time there is later to ensure the outcome of the project is better than expected.

C-suite executives know that time is their most valuable commodity, and everything they do is going to be measured against the amount of time it is going to take. If you are going to be seen as a peer to the C-suite club, you better be ready to accept that each minute of time has a price tag associated with it. What's interesting, too, is that C-suite executives are just as concerned about those around them using their time correctly as they are about using their own time. They adhere to this principle because they know what can happen when someone does not use time efficiently.

Personal Control

People who occupy the C-suite display a certain high level of professionalism in the way they act, talk, dress, and respond to experiences. They know their actions are on display at all times. They know that while what they say and write is important, many times it is how they personally act that speaks loudest. It is only natural, therefore, that people who demonstrate a high degree of personal control are adept at recognizing a similar quality in other people. If a C-suite executive thinks you don't demonstrate a high degree of personal control, then there is an automatic barrier that arises that will forever cloud anything you say. Yes, the C-suite does some stereotyping, but it's no different than what you and I do every day when we encounter people, whether it's in a store, on a street corner, or at a restaurant.

Confidence

This one may seem basic, too, but it is part of the list primarily because I want to define the attribute of confidence as separate from arrogance. Some people shy away from expressing their confidence for fear of being seen as arrogant. The person in the C-suite knows the difference between confidence and arrogance. Senior-level people do not have a problem with confidence. If someone else interprets C-suite executives as being arrogant—when really they are simply being confident—it's the other person's error, not theirs. Allow your confidence to come through when you are meeting with a member of the C-suite club. Failure to display your confidence will quickly result in disconnect between you and the C-suite.

Integrity

Integrity (or the lack thereof) is not only on display publicly in what we say and do, but often becomes most evident in what we *don't say* or *don't do* when no one else is around. People in the C-suite recognize this quality when assessing how someone deals with others. Interestingly, it's not something people can readily identify in themselves. It is far easier to spot integrity in others based on how we see them behave, usually over an extended period of time.

While it takes time to develop integrity, it can take mere seconds to destroy it. View your integrity as a savings account into which you are making contributions on a regular basis, without the intention of ever withdrawing those deposits. Furthermore, do not allow there to be incongruence in how you carry yourself, publicly and privately. The old adage holds true: Your integrity shows up when no one else is watching.

Respect

This plays right into the other traits listed so far. Respect is clearly something people expect from others they come in contact with. Members of the C-suite are accustomed to receiving respect from others; therefore, in their eyes, respect is a nonissue, because they believe everyone should be practicing it. Of course, some people believe you can't show respect *and* be confident at the same time. Members of the C-suite do not see a conflict here. In fact, they believe when the confident person shows the other person respect, it means a lot more. On the other hand, if a person who is not confident attempts to show respect, the C-suite executive will see it as pandering.

Knowledge

Anyone who is looking to communicate with someone in the C-suite must have a strong base of knowledge. For executives, knowledge is not just knowledge about *their* company and *their* industry, but also includes knowledge of geopolitical and business/economic issues. Knowledge, however, is not always exhibited in what you say. Knowledge is also seen in a person's level of confidence in being prepared to handle whatever discussion may arise. You can break down the necessary knowledge into two categories. First, you need to know just enough about most topics to be able to actively participate in and understand a discussion on those topics. Second, you need a deep level of knowledge on the topics that are most important to the C-suite executive.

Trust

Finally, we come to trust, which is the foundation of every other trait C-suite executives expect to see in other people with whom they are going to associate. Without trust, there is no reason for a member of the C-suite to even have a discussion with the other person. The most basic way to prove trustworthiness is whether the parties involved can keep information private. In addition, when it is appropriate to share information with others, it must be done without fluff or exaggeration.

Connecting with the CEO Directly

Pick up your phone and call the CEO with whom you've always wanted to have a meeting. Go ahead and try it and see what happens. In the vast majority of situations, you won't even come close to connecting with the CEO on the phone. In fact, many times you won't connect with anyone even close to the C-suite. Don't worry. Also don't think for a moment that you are not going to be able to get the meeting you want. It just takes time.

Connecting with the CEO or anyone else in the C-suite requires a strategy. It requires a clear understanding of how you intend to break through. There are a number of different approaches, but two of the best ways are by 1) developing a relationship directly with the C-suite member or 2) connecting with the executive by way of a strong referral. You'll notice I'm not saying one of the ways to the C-suite is by working your way up through the organization. This method is by all means the worst and least effective.

I encounter many salespeople who go to great lengths trying to convince me otherwise. They tell me that they've been successful by starting with the one contact they had somewhere in the company and then, through persistence and diligence, working their way up through the organization to a meeting with the CEO. Excuse me for being blunt, but that approach is rarely successful, and if it is successful, it is typically due to a lot of luck and the investment of way too much time. High-profit selling means not only being able to sell at a higher price, but also being able to sell in a time-efficient manner. Salespeople who spend years working their way up through a customer's organization, encountering risk and failure along the way, are certainly not investing their time in an effective manner.

There is a simple reason that approach doesn't work: With each step, you must have a successful sale. If anyone along the way rejects you or your company, you are back to square one. Your odds of being successful are about as likely as trying to throw a ball through several swinging tires at the same time. It's just not going to work. If you want to connect with the CEO or any other person in the C-suite, you need to do it directly, either on your own or through a referral.

The 12 × 12 Approach

Over the years, an effective way I've found to connect with someone in the C-suite is to use what I call the 12 × 12 method. It involves having twelve points of communication over a twelve-month period. Yes, this method takes time, but remember—executives at the C-level will not do business with anyone they don't trust and have confidence in. Confidence and trust take time to build. The 12 × 12 approach requires you to send something of interest to your C-suite contact each month. One month it might be a thank-you letter, expressing gratitude for the person's participation in a charitable event you also support. Another month it might be an e-mail containing a link to an industry article that may be of interest to the C-level executive. Another month it might be a fax with a copy of an article you found in a magazine or daily newspaper that discusses a topic you think will interest the person.

The objective of the monthly communication is to highlight things of interest to the C-suite executive. Don't attempt to make it about you or your company. Certainly *include* your name, company name, and contact information, but do not include a sales brochure or any material about your company.

At this point, the executive is not interested in your company. If you do send material about your company, it could have a negative effect, as the executive may automatically discount any trust in you.

Another tip is to be sure you use different communication methods. Do not always use e-mail, or the telephone, or regular mail. By using different modes of communication, you'll have a better chance of breaking through. Everyone has one or two preferred means of communication. Until you know the preferred method of the person with whom you are trying to connect, you would be wise to use a variety of methods. Remember, too, that you are attempting to reach not only the C-suite contact, but also the executive's gatekeeper. Many times the impression you make on the gatekeeper is going to determine if you even get a meeting with the executive. Members of the C-suite place a high value on time, so it is their gatekeeper's job to carefully screen anything and anyone who may take up some of that time.

After you are about five months into the 12 × 12 process, take the step of calling the C-level person to get an appointment. Chances are you'll get either voice mail or the executive officer's administrative assistant. Either way, it's fine. If you get voice mail, you have at least made another communication contact. Don't expect a call back, but merely continue your monthly habit of communication. If you reach the person's gatekeeper, then you may suddenly find yourself with the opportunity to secure a meeting. The gatekeeper has been seeing your monthly communication, and along the way, has begun to see you as a person who is trying to help, not simply someone trying to sell something.

When talking with the gatekeeper, you should be aware that this person is going to go in one of a few different directions. First, the gatekeeper could reject your request outright. If this happens, don't push it, but rather look to win long term. Thank the gatekeeper for his time and continue with your plan of sending a meaningful form of communication each month.

Second, the gatekeeper may not allow you to have access to the C-suite executive, but instead may refer you to someone else in the company. In this case, politely ask if you could be conference-called with the other person right then to get a meeting. Keeping the gatekeeper on the phone while you talk with the other party will increase your credibility.

Before we get too far along, let me add a few more comments regarding what you should remember if the gatekeeper directs you to someone lower in the company. Your objective is to view these meetings as tryouts for your eventual meeting with the CEO. After each meeting, you are going to make sure the gatekeeper receives from you a report on how the meeting went. If possible, you want to do this follow-up over the phone. Then, make sure you continue to send a monthly communication to the CEO, just as you were doing before your meeting with the person you were referred to by the gatekeeper.

The third route the gatekeeper could take is to allow you to have a meeting with the C-suite executive—which is what you wanted all along. Your key here is to only ask for twenty minutes of the executive's time. I like to use twenty minutes because it's an unusual amount of time and, more than likely, most people will block out thirty minutes on their calendar anyway. You in essence end up with a thirty-minute meeting without asking for thirty minutes, which could appear to be too big of an initial request.

Salespeople around the world have asked me what type of results they can expect from using the 12 × 12 approach. I say your odds of success are much higher than with any other method I've ever seen used. In working with clients across a wide number of industries, I've always been able to achieve a success rate of between 10 percent and 30 percent, typically. The only reason it is not higher is because the salesperson fails to follow through on the monthly commitment to send meaningful information to the C-level executive.

When determining what information to send, use these criteria:

- ► *Industry Information.* News of interest that deals directly with the executive's industry.

- ► *Regulatory Information.* News of pending changes in regulations that may have either a positive or negative impact on the company's executives directly or their industry.

- ► *Congratulatory Information.* A note of congratulations on a personal accomplishment, the company's quarterly earnings, or any other significant piece of information that has been announced.

- ► *Competitive Information.* Anything a competitor is doing that is public information can be shared—as long as you know how the person you are sharing the information with views the competitor. Never speak negatively about a competitor, and also be sure that any information you send won't be construed as being demeaning.

Connecting with the CEO by Way of a Referral

We all would like to have a never-ending supply of referrals to build our business, especially referrals that allow us to be seen by people in the C-suite as one of them. Developing direct relationships with C-suite members isn't always possible. Another viable method of gaining a referral to the C-suite is by developing relationships with other people in the company you are targeting or even with other CEOs by way of social media.

I'm not going to go into a long explanation about how to leverage social media for the simple reason that the rules of social media are changing so quickly, it's impossible to develop any plan and expect it to last for more than a couple of months. What I will say is that you do want to develop relationships through social media sites with other people in the company you are targeting. Use discussion groups and other social media tools to develop these relationships as professional relationships, allowing people to get to know your level of expertise. The objective of this process is to reach the C-suite in a roundabout manner. There is a strong likelihood that, at some point, one of the people with whom you have developed a professional relationship through social media is going to be sitting in a meeting with the CEO, discussing a subject that matches what you can provide, so the person might mention you and suggest a meeting. In that case, your referral to the C-suite is coming by way of your contacts with someone else in the company. This is a much more effective way to reach the C-suite than trying to sell your way up though the company. It's more effective because as you are developing relationships with several people at the same time, you are essentially doing professional marketing as well.

Dealing with the Blockers

You may have a great relationship with the C-level person with whom you are meeting or you may have just started to develop the relationship. In either case, you have to be careful of those people who will look to obstruct you and your strategy to sell to the C-suite. I refer to these people as the "blockers." Sometimes you'll know who they are and sometimes you won't. More often than not, the blockers will be people you will never meet. To make matters worse, sometimes the blockers don't even know what it is you are trying to sell. Blockers take on all forms and all causes, but for the most part, they can be broken down into three different types:

- ▶ People who say "no" to everything.

- ▶ People who are always looking to turn every situation into an opportunity from which they can personally benefit.

> ► People who are looking to block you in favor of a competing solution.

Let's look more closely at each one of these types.

The first type of blocker—the person who says "no," no matter what, is often from the finance department or another analytical-type department. These blockers tend to base their views on the argument that they don't have all the facts. They want to study any idea until it's no longer worth studying and the opportunity goes away. These people can be extremely detrimental to a corporation when it comes to exploring new ideas and opportunities. Avoid having them impede your progress by being very up-front in your discussions with the C-suite. Be sure you have a clear understanding of how decisions are made and what information is necessary to make the final decision. Leverage time in these situations so that you can work to close the sale rapidly by emphasizing the strategic importance of making the decision. Of utmost importance is keeping these blockers from having anything more than a low-level involvement in the decision-making process.

In the second category are blockers who use every situation to help make themselves look good. When you spot one of these people, play to their ego and allow them to be involved. Give them something they can personally win. Don't attempt to work around them. If you do, you run the risk of having the decision-making process spin completely out of control. You may still wind up with the sale, but the chances are high that the sale will come with a number of other criteria attached to it that will hurt your bottom-line profit.

The last type of blocker is the person who is blocking your proposal out of the belief that a competing proposal is better. In that situation, the solution lies in your ability to sell. When I say "sell," I do not mean applying hard-core pressure. I mean allowing everyone associated with the C-suite to see and understand the full value of your offer. Keep in mind that as important as it is to be selling to the C-suite with the expectation that the executives are the ones who will make the buying decision, you also must remember there are others in the company who will undoubtedly be providing input to the C-suite.

Meeting with the CEO

Your work has paid off, and on your calendar is the meeting you have wanted with the CEO or other C-suite members. This meeting should not be one where you lay out all of your capabilities and dazzle them with slick presentations. Instead, your focus should be on engaging the C-suite members in a serious discussion that allows them to see you as being strategically oriented. In this meeting you now have the opportunity to demonstrate confidence and build trust thanks to all of the work you have done communicating with the C-suite in getting them to even meet with you. Your goal is for the person you are meeting with to see you as a strategic thinker he or she can rely on. This is extremely important, because if you allow the discussion to become tactical in nature—asking about specific dates, operational issues, and other intricate details—you will run the risk of being referred down in the organization to somebody at a much lower level. C-suite members won't welcome questions that are seen as either beneath their level or ones they know they can't answer. High performers in the C-suite are always looking for ways to get things off of their plate; therefore, it's important the C-suite members see your questions and comments as being both strategic in nature and intellectually driven to provoke their thinking.

Always view your meeting with anyone in the C-suite as a discussion that will be continued with either another meeting or via e-mail or telephone. I don't mean that you should not push for decisions to be made when you are in the meeting. On the contrary, when you are in the C-suite, the expectation is for you to ask for the order and ask quickly. However, if you adopt the view that discussions need to continue, you'll have a better opportunity to develop a meaningful relationship with the C-suite executive.

Several of the rules to which I subscribe with junior-level employees apply just the same in a senior-level meeting. First, if you can't close the sale, at least gain agreement on something. Second, never leave without a clear next step, and the next step should include a specific date for something to occur. Agreeing on a specific date for some follow-up correspondence or phone call allows the C-suite person to assess your follow-up skills. Of course, responding by the agreed-upon time is actually responding too late. Always look to beat the delivery date. Your ability to consistently be early will raise the level of confidence senior-level executives have in you.

Selling to the C-suite is a highly effective sales strategy; however, it should not be seen as your only sales strategy, except in those rare situations where what you sell requires C-suite involvement. The timeline required to penetrate and close a sale with the C-suite can be two to four times longer than your normal sales strategy. Without proper planning, it's very possible you'll have little to show in your sales pipeline in the end. The best way to use the C-suite strategy is as one of many strategies you have at your command to make your quarterly and annual numbers. Even if you already have a solid relationship and profitable business with a customer, it still makes sense to develop relationships with the C-suite. In these situations the relationship with the C-suite can be viewed as both an insurance policy and an extended research department.

C-Suite Relationships Are Insurance Policies

Like an insurance policy, a C-suite relationship should already be there when you need it, should problems crop up and you or someone else from your company need assistance from a senior-level person. The last thing you want to do is to try and build a relationship with senior management in the midst of a crisis. If this happens, you will have to spend an inordinate amount of extra time working to get the issues resolved compared to the salesperson who has relationships already in place.

C-Suites Are Research Departments

When you have a solid relationship already in place with the occupants of the C-suite, you typically have the opportunity to learn key information about the customer. Often the C-suite will use outside suppliers as a sounding board for information, and information winds up flowing both ways. Your opinion may be sought for assistance on an issue of interest to the customer that only those in the C-suite have knowledge of. If you are able to be part of those discussions, you are then in a position to be among the first to know where the customer is headed. The end result is the knowledge you acquire can significantly help increase your level of sales with the company.

C-suite relationships are without a doubt essential if you are truly going to be selling at a high-profit margin. Failure to develop relationships at that level will nearly always result in profitable dollars being left on the table.

How to Handle Price Objections

M ANY TIMES SALESPEOPLE deliver a great sales presentation. They engage the customer and do a wonderful job of understanding the customer's needs and desired benefits. When it appears they have everything going for them in order to close the sale, the customer suddenly throws out a comment or makes a statement that leaves the salesperson speechless.

Sometimes the statement is as simple as, "Your price is too high." Other times it can be a more complicated objection, but the meaning is the same—the customer is looking for a discount. No matter how the objection is raised, salespeople usually have a common response: They start thinking the sale might not happen.

When you are confronted with this situation, the challenge is in how you choose to respond. If you respond in the right manner and maintain control, you will successfully close the sale. If, on the other hand, you allow the customer to get the best of you, you'll either lose the sale completely or close the sale at a reduced profit. All of the training in the world cannot prepare you for every selling situation you may face. The best you can do is be as prepared as possible to handle the situation if the customer throws you a price-centered objection.

In this chapter I'll show you how to overcome the threats and demands a customer can make regarding price. I'll even share how many times the best way to respond to the price objection is by not responding at all.

You should always keep in mind that just because a sale *can* be made doesn't mean it is necessarily a good sale. A good sale is when you make a decent profit and the customer's needs and desired benefits are met. Too often it's the customer who wins at the expense of the salesperson, all because the salesperson failed to handle the price objection properly.

You Need to Be Blunt with the Customer

Each year I make a number of international trips to speak to groups on the subject of sales and how to maximize price. As popular as the topic is in the United States, it's even more popular in other countries. One time I had a call from Asia where the person wanted to talk to me about speaking at an upcoming conference in his country. The conversation was going well, typical of discussions I have with people both in the United States and abroad. Then came a statement I've heard far too many times: *You'll give me your best friend price, won't you?* Each time I hear this line or any variation of it, I have to laugh. In every case, the person making the comment is someone I've never met and with whom I have no relationship. Hearing this request triggers my automatic response, "I don't have a best friend price, and I don't know you, so even if I did have a best friend price, I wouldn't give it to you." Is it blunt? Yes, but that's the point.

The first rule of dealing with a price objection is for you to be confident and straightforward with the customer. If there is any hesitation on your part, it will just make the customer even more determined to get a lower price. A rule I like to follow is that if the customer is going to be blunt with me in asking about price, I'll be blunt with the customer in return. Maybe this directness stems from my time selling in New York City, but no matter where I developed the strategy, I've found it works.

I've watched too many salespeople become visibly shaken when they hear comments from customers regarding price that I would hardly deem threatening. No wonder so many customers ask for a lower price. They often get it without even trying very hard. If the salesperson is going to cave to the demands of the customer who is barely asking, how much more will the salesperson cave when the customer gets assertive and forceful?

When I share this perspective with salespeople, I often get push back. They say that if they aren't willing to at least work with a customer, then they soon won't have any customers at all. To me, this is a very bad assumption, and one that results in both short- and long-term problems. The short-term problem is the customer immediately gets a lower price. The long-term problem, which I have discussed in other chapters, is that going forward, the customer now has a lower perception of the value of what the salesperson is selling.

How Should You Respond to Objections?

Objections to price can come in a number of ways. Sometimes it's the straightforward statement regarding price. Other times customers hide their concern about price and instead throw out an objection about something else. In both cases, how you respond is going to determine the profitability of the sale, if there is even a sale to be made. Let me again say that it's important to be blunt with the customer. When you are blunt with the customer, it shows your confidence. However, it's also important for you to frame your response in a manner similar to how the customer posed the objection.

If a customer cautiously makes a statement regarding price, then your sudden and forceful response of "No" will answer the objection, while also turning the customer off from buying anything. The proper response in this scenario should be to use a manner and tone only slightly firmer than the tone and manner the customer used when making the statement. In this manner, you are still able to get your point across without turning off the customer. The key is to respond to the price objection but to keep the discussion moving forward so that you can ultimately close the sale.

It is not unusual for a new customer to ask for the price before even beginning any discussion with the salesperson. The customer may, for instance, send out mass e-mails to numerous suppliers, asking them to forward their price list. Other times the request may come from the administrative assistant of someone who is clearly not authorized to buy. These people are charged with contacting a prospective salesperson to give the illusion a big sale could be made because they ask for pricing. In both of these situations, as soon as you offer up any pricing information, you lose. You lose in two ways. First, if you offer up any type of a price, the customer now has the ability to establish a benchmark price from which to negotiate, limiting your profit potential. Second, the price can be used as a disqualifier, eliminating the opportunity for the salesperson to even have a discussion with the decision maker.

Salespeople may say they do not respond to these kind of queries, but they occur more frequently than we all believe. Even if you haven't dealt with one of the exact scenarios I've described, you likely are receiving quick phone calls from a lower-level person in a company who asks about the availability of a particular product and then quickly asks what the price is. This strategy is employed successfully by many purchasing departments. The reason it works so well is that the customer is able to get the salesperson talking about something, and before you know it, the salesperson unknowingly gives out a price as a way to demonstrate customer service.

Anytime you encounter any of these situations or anything even similar to them, you need to respond to the customer firmly, saying that it is not possible to know what the price is because of a number of factors. At that point, you need to immediately start asking critical questions that only the decision maker would be able to answer. Your goal here is to demonstrate to the person who is trying to get pricing information—but likely is not the decision maker—that it is paramount that the decision maker be involved. If the customer continues to push for pricing information, you then should state that it is not your company's policy to release pricing information until a customer profile document has been completed on the prospective customer. The customer profile document is simply the basic information regarding the customer, along with the answers you get to the questions you initially ask the customer.

Over the years, I've found that if a customer refuses to share information with the salesperson before receiving any pricing information, the customer is not worth the interaction. I take a hard line here because it is too easy for salespeople to give in to the requests of a customer. In the end, the only thing the salesperson winds up with is a low-margin customer.

Responding to the Request for a Reduction in Price

One of the most common questions I'm asked anytime I'm with salespeople is: What is the best way to respond to a customer's request for a lower price or a customer's statement that the price is too high? My answer is simple. Don't respond to the question. You read that right—when customers ask you for a reduction in price, you should simply ignore them. Now that I have your attention, let me explain.

When customers ask for a lower price, it's important to first determine if they mean what they are saying or if they are merely saying what they *believe* they should be saying. The best way for you to find out how serious the customer is regarding a reduction in price is to ignore the customer's initial comment. Surprisingly, just overlooking the comment the first time the customer makes it will take care of some of these requests for a lower price. The key is to not even flinch when the customer asks for the discount, but rather continue on with the sales presentation. The confidence you show will eliminate the customer who is timidly asking for a better price. Only if the customer brings up the issue of a price reduction a second time should you respond. However, your response should not be a direct reply to the customer's request for a lower price, but should take the form of another question. Ask the customer a question directed at the most important need the customer is looking to solve. Your objective in asking customers this type of question is to get them thinking about what it is they need to solve in the first place. Directing attention to their most critical need puts their focus on something else instead of lowering the price. This approach of turning attention from price toward need will remove the pricing barrier from another group of customers.

In working with thousands of salespeople on this technique, I'm pleased to say the results are much better than most salespeople initially believe they will be. Yes, the results vary by industry and the type of buyer with whom the salesperson is dealing, but in all cases, the results are positive. In my experience, there are two factors that affect the results salespeople get from this response: their body language when they encounter the price objection and how they immediately respond to the customer's first and second request for a price reduction. Salespeople who do not allow their body language or tone of voice to reflect any hesitation are the ones who have the most success with this approach. On the other hand, the salesperson who hesitates when the customer poses the price reduction question is the one who generally is the least successful.

Just because you're dealing with a customer over the telephone does not mean your body language is not important. Yes, the customer may not be able to see you but what that means is your tone of voice is even more important. Surprising to many people is how body language comes through in the voice. The discussion may be taking place on the telephone but that does not discount the need for ensuring your body language communicates you are in control. One of the best ways to do this is by standing up anytime you are dealing with a customer regarding a pricing issue. Standing up will naturally give you more firmness in your voice, which will translate to confidence in how it is heard.

It bears repeating that the best approach to overcome any hesitation is for you to always be ready with a critical question you can ask that deals with the customer's most critical need. You prepare by listening carefully and writing down each key need or benefit you hear the customer mention during the sales call. For each need or benefit you hear the customer share, you should also write down a question you could ask if necessary. In other words, you are using the information the customer is sharing early in the sales call to help you not only close the sale later, but also defend yourself should the need arise from issues such as price. By taking notes during the sales call and having the question ready in advance, you will be more confident.

What Do You Do About the Persistent Customer?

As you probably already know, there are customers who are going to be persistent in asking for or virtually demanding a price reduction before they will buy. These customers still provide you with the opportunity to close a sale at a profit, but only if you use caution in how you show value to the customer. If you are dealing with a professional buyer, you may find yourself at a stalemate in not being able to move the sale forward until you address price. Even if the customer is not a professional buyer, there are still those customers who will be unyielding in demanding a reduction in price. At this point, you, as the salesperson, have two options.

One option is to firmly state that there are no adjustments to price, and with that statement, be fully prepared to end the sales call. This approach definitely takes a lot of confidence on your part and on the part of your superior. Your boss, after all, is going to have to support you with the level of confidence necessary to enable you to walk away from a sale that is not full price. I highly recommend this approach when you know the customer has a critical need and the time for the customer to make a decision is running short. The vital point in this approach is that the customer is on a timeline. This is why it is so important early in a sales call to learn the customer's timeline and process for making a decision. When you know these things, you are in a much better position to respond correctly to the customer, should you suddenly hear an objection regarding price.

The second option you can take with a persistent customer is to ask what the customer wants in terms of a price reduction. I recommend this approach only after you have ignored the customer's request the first time and if you don't know enough about the customer's needs and decision-making timeline. This second approach is not the preferred approach. Once you ask about the amount of price reduction the customer is looking for, you must be ready to respond with a comment that emphasizes an important benefit you believe the customer will see as value. You then must follow the statement with an engaging question that gets the customer talking about the benefit you just mentioned. You must listen for how intensely the customer stresses price compared to how intensely he speaks of the benefit. Your goal is to convince the customer that you, the salesperson, understand his desire to receive better value. But at the same time—and this is the key point—you cannot allow the customer to think the better value is going to come in the form of a reduced price. If the customer still believes that he is going to get a lower price, you have lost control of the sales call.

The number one thing you must remember in order to maintain control of the sales call is to give the customer plenty of eye contact. If you are not looking the customer squarely in the eye, any smart customer will know you are not confident in what you're saying and there is room for a reduction in price.

Getting Customers to Focus on Their Needs, Not Your Price

I cannot stress enough the importance of showing customers the value in what they are looking to buy from you. If customers still believe they are going to receive a lower price based on their request, again I recommend that you strongly reiterate that the price is firm. You must hold firm on price because—and here's the important part—customers who are concerned only about low price are not the type of customers you want to have. When customers argue too much about price before a sale is even close to being made, then they are probably going to argue over everything after the sale. Let me repeat what I've been saying all along: Salespeople who sell only to customers who are focused on low price are not salespeople; they are nothing more than order takers.

If the customer cannot grasp the benefits of what they are looking to buy, then there is no sense for you to continue dealing with them. Unfortunately, many salespeople keep on wasting their time dealing with customers who have little potential to generate a profit for them. The sooner you walk away from the customer who is focused solely on low price, the better off both parties will be. I can't tell you the number of times in my sales career when I've found myself initially excited about closing a sale with a customer who was 100 percent focused on obtaining the lowest price, only to later regret that I ever made the sale in the first place. The regret sets in because the customer continues fighting, challenging, and arguing over every little thing once the sale is made. The level of additional support required to keep this customer happy wipes out whatever small profit was gained. This type of situation can quickly create an entirely new set of problems that, in most cases, is only corrected when the customer is no longer a customer.

It's not unusual to have customers who will ask for a price reduction before they place their first order and then actually still complain about the price! These types of customers can be quite common in some industries. It's important for you to have a proven strategy to prevent their constant requests from chipping away at your profit.

When dealing with these types of customers, the first thing you must do is to verify their key needs. This includes understanding the benefits they want and the risks they are facing. The more information you have, the more equipped you will be to deal with their ongoing requests. I recommend that each time you communicate with the customer, you start the conversation by asking a question regarding one of the customer's major concerns. By going on the offense, you are in a position to be able to get such customers talking about their own problems. The objective, of course, is to have them thinking more about the issues they are facing than thinking about asking you for a lower price.

A few years ago I was working with a firm that sold software in a very competitive sector. This company was accustomed to selling to customers who regularly did return-on-investment studies on any software they purchased. The company did offer its clients a favorable return on investment; however, it was not that much different from what other software vendors offered. Customers would challenge the vendor to offer a lower price, especially if they began to factor in the annual service and licensing agreements. The sales management team and I were able to forecast out a few years and see margins continuing to decrease because of how the return on investment looked for customers. The solution was to reframe the software's value proposition. We changed the focus from helping to save labor to minimizing risk. Yes, customers saved labor costs by using the software, but more important, they eliminated a critical risk to their operations. Although the risk customers eliminated was not very likely to occur, if it did, they would incur significant losses, some of which they might never be able to overcome. After retraining the sales force, the software company was able to significantly reduce the number of challenges it was facing from customers looking for a lower price, since those customers were now building their return-on-investment analysis around an entirely different set of criteria.

This example shows how you can direct the customer's focus away from price if you understand enough about the customer's needs, desired benefits, and risks. If you attempt to deal with the customer who is continually looking for a discount without knowing enough about the customer, you will have little chance of holding on to the customer without discounting price.

The Customer Is in No Rush to Buy

Salespeople ask me all the time how they should deal with the customer who is not in a rush to buy, and I tell them there are two things they can do. First, don't be in a rush to sell to the customer who is not in a rush to buy. Second, have a full pipeline of prospective customers. Let me build on both of these points, starting with the second point.

A full pipeline of prospects naturally gives salespeople a level of confidence that allows them to be more resistant to the numerous requests a customer may throw at them, especially involving price. I'm a firm believer that no matter how much business you may currently be doing as a salesperson, you should still spend a portion of your selling day prospecting. I am not, however, a believer in the strategy of a key account manager having only one customer. Salespeople who have only one customer run the risk of the customer skillfully manipulating them. Often, the salesperson doesn't even see the manipulation coming. If the lone customer suddenly runs into issues, the key account manager will begin to scramble in a way that quickly can put his company's bottom-line profit at risk. Spending a portion of each day—or at least a portion of each week—on prospecting is essential to the salesperson's peace of mind. It gives salespeople the prospects they need to prevent them from thinking they have only one major customer to depend on for sales.

Now, let's deal with your other option. If the customer is in no rush to buy, then you shouldn't be in a rush to sell. I can't emphasize this point enough. If you want to maximize profits, you must sell to the customer's timeline, not your own. Anytime you attempt to close a sale based on your own timeline, you run the risk of giving up profit. This doesn't mean you can't do things that can help accelerate the buyer's decision-making process. You must, however, be careful that you are not speeding up the decision at the expense of profit.

If you want to speed up the customer's decision making, the best way is to focus your presentation on those needs, desired benefits, or risks that are associated with deadlines or time. Years ago, one of my customers was in no rush to buy several new items I had been trying to convince him to buy. The items were merely replacements for other items, so the buyer was not going to place an order until his existing inventory was depleted. Although I knew I'd eventually get an order, I also knew it would be at least six months away. Obviously, that wasn't going to help my quarterly numbers.

I finally was able to get the customer to place an order with me four months ahead of his timetable by successfully convincing him of the risk his company would face by waiting until the existing inventory was gone. In this case, I showed the customer how a low inventory level would potentially cause serious disruption if the existing product failed or became obsolete. In my comparison, I shared with the buyer how the cost of buying the new items from me now was a small investment in comparison to the risk the company might incur. This strategy allowed me to close the sale and maintain profit margins for both of us. The profit margin the customer received by buying early was the confidence in knowing he had eliminated a potential risk for his company. If I had not chosen this approach, the only way I could have closed the sale would have been to offer the buyer a discount large enough to encourage him to make a purchase. This certainly would have allowed the customer to eliminate risk of product failure or obsolescence, but it would have been at the sacrifice of profit on my part.

Some people might say the buyer simply didn't push enough. Possibly, but I think the customer realized the risk was real and he needed to face it. The two things that allowed me to close the sale at the full margin were my explanation of the risk and my unwillingness to bend on price. From the first sales call all the way through to the close, something the customer never saw me do was discount the price. This story illustrates why I believe so strongly in maintaining a strong stance toward price all the way through the sales process. From early in the selling process, smart customers are ready to take your measure, and they will pick up on your every movement or comment. As much as these things can work against you when it comes time to close, they can also work for you in helping to maintain profits.

Don't Try to Push the Customer with a Limited-Time Discount

A tactic used by too many companies to drive sales with customers who are not in a rush to buy is to offer some sort of price discount for a limited time. The automotive industry uses this strategy with consumers more than probably any other industry. Automakers are also a perfect example to illustrate how detrimental this approach can be on an entire industry. Sure, many others in the business-to-consumer environment also use this practice, but it exists in the business-to-business environment, too. The only difference is that B2B discounting to spur along customers who aren't quite ready to buy goes on quietly and without the same fanfare that's evident in consumer-oriented industries.

This book is not the place to discuss all of the implications of creating short-term sales by targeting customers who are in no rush to buy. There are certainly numerous financial reasons why it might make sense for a company to offer a discount to encourage sales at the end of fiscal quarter or year. To keep this book from expanding to a thousand pages, I'll leave that issue alone.

When you attempt to use a discounted price to encourage a sale from customers who are in no rush to buy, you may wind up with a sale. Unfortunately, you will have simultaneously forever changed the price/value relationship customers have in their mind. Professional buyers often use this in-no-rush-to-buy tactic as a way of getting a discount. They will let the salesperson believe they are in no rush to buy, all the while knowing they need to place an order soon. Time is an amazing tool that both customers and salespeople can use to help close a sale. The earlier you can find out the timeline in which the customer is going to make a decision, the less likely it remains on the table as a tool the customer potentially could use to get a discount.

Sell First, Negotiate Second

I want to make one final comment before wrapping up this chapter. You'll notice that I have resisted using the words *negotiation* or *negotiating*. I'm a firm believer that we need to sell first and negotiate second. Too many salespeople give up a tremendous amount of profit by being willing to negotiate with customers far too early in the sales process. No negotiations should take place with a customer until the customer has rejected your offer on two separate occasions. My reasoning is simple: You cannot negotiate anything successfully unless you know what it is you are negotiating. Any salesperson who attempts to negotiate too early is doomed to lose.

Waiting until the offer has been rejected twice gives you the opportunity to learn what the customer's key needs, desired benefits, and risks are. It allows you to understand how the customer communicates and what the customer's timeline is for making a decision. There are a host of other things you can and will learn if you take the time to sell. If you truly listen to the customer, you will be able to close the sale without having to negotiate anything. When you close the sale without negotiating, you then have the best opportunity to sell at the highest profit possible.

CHAPTER 12

Executing a Price Increase

FEW THINGS IN SALES can be more difficult than having to tell a customer there will be an increase in price. Although it's difficult for the salesperson, it can be one of the most important steps a company can take. Instituting a price increase is not something any company does without a lot of thought, but even after all of the preparation for taking a price increase, too often it fails to stick. One problem that arises is that customers push back and threaten to take their business elsewhere. The end result is the additional profit that was expected due to the increase in price fails to materialize.

A price increase also can fail if the sales force doesn't know how to present it properly. This is a real problem, and I think it is a much bigger issue than most companies are willing to admit. I've received numerous phone calls from companies asking for assistance in figuring out a plan to get customers to accept an increase in price. In the majority of these scenarios, what I discover is that the real issue is with the sales force, not with the price increase itself.

Based on my work with many companies, I've developed a ten-step process companies should follow when looking to increase their prices. The beauty of the ten-step process is that it addresses how to ensure success both with the customer and with the sales force. Too often senior management attempts to place immediate demands on the sales force with the expectation that everything will be handled in no time at all. The ten-step process is designed to prevent that type of problem.

Certainly there are times when a price increase needs to be executed with little or no lead time; however, those types of situations are far fewer than many people believe. Even in those situations where lead time is short, the ten-step process still can be an effective tool in preventing major problems with customers or salespeople.

The Ten-Step Process to Execute a Price Increase

First, let's list the ten steps. Following this list, I will detail each step.

1. Know your strategy as to what the price increase is going to accomplish, and establish expectations and goals.

2. Sell the objective the price increase is designed to accomplish to those people inside the company, particularly the sales force.

3. Determine and isolate the customer's key benefits, as these help sell the price increase.

4. Understand the customer's decision-making timeline and how it may impact your plans to communicate the price increase.

5. Isolate key contacts within the customer's company.

6. Develop data and a fact-driven point of view (FDPOV).

7. Signal to the customer the expectation that a price increase might be coming.

8. Formalize expectations and goals with the sales force for each customer.

9. Present the price increase to customers and gain their commitment.

10. Reinforce the price increase by sharing the FDPOV.

No step can be left out. Each step is designed to help with the next step. Think of the ten steps as an iceberg. The largest portion of the iceberg is below the surface and not visible to anyone. In our price increase process, steps 1 through 6 are below the water; steps 7 and 8 are at the waterline; and, finally, steps 9 and 10 are clearly visible to everyone.

Using the ten-step process does not guarantee success, but it will increase the success rate significantly. The ten steps have been designed to ensure the sales force is involved in the planning. Involving the sales force in the planning is essential if your salespeople are going to buy into the idea of the price increase and understand their role in the process. (*Note*: It is equally important that both sales managers and salespeople understand the ten-step process.)

Now, let's detail each step.

Step 1: Know Your Strategy and What the Price Increase Is Going to Accomplish

The reasons for implementing a price increase can vary. One company may take a price increase because of increases it is receiving from its suppliers, while another company may take an increase solely as a way to increase profit. Some companies base their price increases on what their competitors are charging. In these situations, an increase may come immediately after a major competitor has taken a price increase.

Regardless of the reason, a company must develop an overall strategy for what the price increase is going to accomplish. After the strategy is set, objectives must then be developed for how the price increase is going to be carried out and a general timeline established for when it will be done.

The strategy must include information that will allow the sales force to buy into the increase. The strategy can be broad or concise, but must be done with the expectation that management will communicate the price increase to salespeople in a manner that allows them to understand the rationale for the increase.

Define the Rationale for the Increase

The increase in price can be based on virtually anything, as long as there is factual information to support the reasons. Taking an increase based on future expectations is certainly a viable strategy. In my work with companies, I strongly recommend not basing an increase solely on what has already happened to costs in the past. I am also a strong advocate of making sure any price increase takes into consideration the expectation of future increases in costs. I refer to it as *forward pricing*. If no planning is done to take into account future increases in costs, then the vendor will always be in a situation where it is not achieving the profit margins it expects.

Here is an example of forward pricing:

Historical Manufacturing Cost:	$10.00 per unit
Historical Selling Cost:	$14.00 per unit
Historical Profit:	$4.00 per unit: 28.6% margin
Current Manufacturing Cost:	$12.00
Current Selling Cost:	$14.00
Current Profit:	$ 2.00 per unit: 14.3% margin
Projected Future Manufacturing Cost:	$13.00 per unit

If the company does not take into account projected future manufacturing cost when planning for the current price increase, it will find itself having to take a second increase just to stay even. The preferred plan is to take one increase that reflects what the future increases in cost might be for production.

In this example, the forward-pricing action would be to increase the price by $3.00 per unit, if it is to be a dollar-for-dollar increase. This takes into consideration the difference between the historical manufacturing cost and the projected future manufacturing cost $1.00 forward-pricing action needed. If the strategy is to retain the same margin, then the planned increase should be $5.20, which would allow the company to remain at the 28.6 percent margin.

Any discussion among senior management regarding a price increase must include the concept of forward pricing.

Develop the Information to Support the Increase

Once the strategy has been developed and the price increase has been determined, it is essential to share information with the sales force. The information that's developing at this step is not necessarily shared with any customers, though. The sole purpose of the information is to help the sales force understand the reason for the increase.

Senior managers sometime believe it is not necessary to share information with the sales force. They may think sharing this type of information is not important or they may feel the information is too sensitive to share. Both of these reasons will jeopardize the expected outcome of the price increase.

The type of information gathered does not have to be restricted to only internal data. Often the best information is based on the industry in general or even the overall economy. If the price increase is designed to help increase profit margins, you might include information gathered from publicly traded companies that are similar to yours. If the expected increase in profit margins is likely to be seen as excessive, don't try to hide it. If salespeople feel information is being withheld from them, their skepticism will grow. My experience has shown that as the skepticism of a company's salespeople grows, the results they achieve will fall. Large profit margins are the goal of any company, and this type of information should be shared with the sales force, with the expectation that the large margins help ensure continued success. Whatever the reason for the increase, there is information that management can—and should—share with the sales force.

Establish the Expectations and Goals

Some people would argue it is not possible to set the goals without the plan being fully developed, and yes, this is partially true. Although finalizing goals is not possible at this step, it is still necessary to establish the overall goal and expectation of what the price increase is going to accomplish—in particular, what it is going to contribute to the company's top line and bottom line. (Step 8 takes the overall objectives, established in step 1, and breaks them down to the individual customer level.) Along with the expected increase in profit, dates must be established at this phase for when the price increase will be taken and when customers will be asked to sign on to the increase. The dates selected will naturally impact the expected profit, which is why the profit increase and the date must be determined at the same time. Too many companies have missed their quarterly profit targets because of overly optimistic expectations of a price increase being accepted by all customers on the same day without any fallout.

Step 2: Sell the Objective of the Price Increase to People Inside the Company, Particularly the Sales Force

Successfully implementing this step will do more to ensure the success of the price increase than any other step. The sales force and each person who has any contact with customers must be part of this phase. Completion of this step happens when all of the employees who deal with customers have bought into the rationale for the increase.

The biggest requirement here is to allow the sales force the opportunity to respond to the planned increase. Merely sending each member of the sales team a memo listing the reasons for the increase is not good enough. The best people to carry out this phase are the sales managers themselves. This, of course, means they first have to buy into the reason for the sales increase. I have encountered many situations where the sales manager has not bought into the need for an increase. When this occurs, there is no doubt the sales team members under that person will not execute the increase properly. Each person must buy into the process, which means allowing each person the opportunity to challenge the reasons and discuss the pros and cons of the price increase. It is important for salespeople to share their issues. The earlier their issues are brought into the open, the faster they can be addressed. This is why the gathering of information to support the increase in step 1 is so important.

People ask me how to handle salespeople who do not want to accept an increase. My response is to first allow the salespeople to share all of their concerns and for the sales manager to address them as best he can, using the data developed in step 1. After the sales manager has done all he can with the data, the sales manager must demonstrate good leadership and clarify the objectives to the salespeople. The sales manager must also clearly tell salespeople to go out and execute it.

Ultimately, it is the responsibility of members of the sales force to carry out the tasks with which they are charged. I don't say this to minimize the need to share with them the reasons for the price increase and the information to support it. I say this because there are some people who will never accept the reason, and for those salespeople, the only solution is to clearly tell them to do what they are supposed to do. People have asked me if I feel those who are ordered to execute a price increase achieve poorer results than those who believe in the increase. My answer is yes—people who believe in the increase will almost always deliver better results, which is why step 2 is so critical.

Step 3: Determine and Isolate the Customer's Key Benefits (They Help Sell the Price Increase)

After the reasons for the price increase have been shared with the salespeople, they are then in the position to determine the customer's significant needs. The more critical the needs the customer has, the greater success the salesperson will have with the price increase. If salespeople can't identify critical needs, they should focus on identifying the customer's goals or a few key issues they can concentrate on with the customer. When the salesperson can focus on helping the customer solve these critical needs or issues, the customer will begin to see this salesperson as being more knowledgeable and therefore more important than most other salespeople.

If a salesperson anticipates the customer is going to resist the price increase, one strategy the salesperson can use is to do a test or study with the customer. The test or study should focus on something of importance to the customer. It should also be structured for a length of time that will extend beyond when the price increase is going to take effect. One example of this might be a transportation company testing different delivery times for a customer. A software company might arrange a test of different software configurations to allow a customer to measure changes in productivity.

Implementing a test with a customer can serve as a buffer when it comes time to present the increase. If the test or project is truly important to the customer, then there is no way the customer would threaten to stop buying from the salesperson based on a price increase by itself. Implementing this tactic with the customer can be an effective way to help mitigate having to deal with an irate customer making such threats. Even if a study or test is not done, it is still important for the salesperson to discuss critical needs with the customer on every call. The sooner these discussions can begin, the more time the salesperson will have to create in the mind of the customer the important role the salesperson plays. Again, the tactic is doing everything possible to be seen as a critical asset the customer can't live without.

Step 4: Understand the Customer's Decision-Making Timeline and How It May Impact Plans to Communicate the Price Increase

All customers have timelines they use for various projects. A customer that is a reseller may have a cycle built around when it releases new catalogs to its customers. A customer that is a manufacturer or assembler of items for others may have an annual contract or internal budget process it goes through. These are just two examples, but nearly every customer has defined processes associated with running its business.

Understanding the customer's business cycle is essential information for every salesperson. For instance, there may be key dates or periods when a discussion with the customer on pricing might be more ideally suited, so you might strive to coordinate your timing of an increase to those periods. Key dates may include knowing when a customer sets their annual plan or budget. Other key dates could be product launch events or their fiscal quarter dates.

Although it is not always possible to fit the timing of a price increase around every customer's business cycle, it can be helpful on several levels. It helps the salesperson be better prepared for issues that may arise and to determine how to best use her own time. It also can help sales managers know when certain customers may require more involvement on their part.

Even though I believe knowing a customer's timeline is important, I do not think a vendor should automatically adjust the timing of a price increase to fit the timeline of every customer. That would be virtually impossible and would set the sales force up for potential problems if the industry cannot handle multiple pricing options. Some industries and products can handle different pricing for every customer while other industries, including those that are highly regulated, are not able to offer pricing variances. I do, however, believe it makes good sense to set the timing of the increase around the timeline of the one or two major customers whose business accounts for a large sum of revenue. The downside to this approach is that if these customers are in a competitive industry where companies are able to watch closely what each is doing, it could create a backlash among other customers.

Step 5: Isolate Key Contacts Within the Customer's Company

This step is as much about defense as it is offense. While salespeople are expected to already have excellent relationships with numerous people who work for the customer, there is always room to improve the customer relationship. The salesperson should use the weeks or months leading up to a price increase to meet with as many customer contacts as possible.

Some of these meetings should also involve other helpful people the salesperson can bring to the customer. Examples of other helpful people could include logistics, finance, design, research, and development. For the salesperson it is an opportunity to position his company as a knowledge expert the customer cannot live without. This could be referred to as the offense.

The defense part of this step is in being able to tap the good relationships that are in place should issues arise when the salesperson is communicating the price increase to the customer. Having existing relationships with all of the key people in a customer's company can help salespeople who find themselves having to defend the merits of the price increase with others besides the buyer with whom they normally work. Additionally, having contacts with as many people as possible gives the salesperson more credibility with the buyer. This shows up in the buyer's belief that the salesperson is a key partner to the buyer's company.

Step 6: Develop Data and a Fact-Driven Point of View (FDPOV)

Fact-driven point of view is a term I first developed when doing consulting with several major companies. FDPOV is all about preparing a company's salespeople by supplying them with the information and story they can use with their customers to help communicate the reasons for the price increase. This step must be carried out by the individual salesperson, but with the support of marketing, finance, support, and others inside the company who provide the salesperson with information.

The objective is for salespeople to have available facts they trust and can use with the customer to help explain the merits of the price increase. The best facts are those that support or help the customer deal with their critical needs. When the facts shared with the customers are of importance to the customers, they will be much more ready to accept them.

The "point of view" portion of FDPOV is the salesperson's point of view. Anytime people share their own point of view, they do so with much more passion and force than if they were merely sharing information. Presenting the salesperson's point of view is important because it increases the power of the message being relayed to the customer.

In my experience, this step is the most time-consuming one and cannot be rushed. The message will change for each customer, so it is essential for the salesperson to have the time and resources to develop the message. On occasion the FDPOV may change by the time the salesperson is ready to take it to the customer in steps 9 and 10. It may change only because of new insights the salesperson is able to obtain as they carry out steps 7 and 8.

Step 7: Signal to the Customer the Expectation That a Price Increase Might Be Coming

Some people will say it is not good practice to let customers know a price increase is coming in advance of the official price increase announcement. Although this is true to some extent, I also believe it is the responsibility of a salesperson to give customers (existing customers in particular) as much lead time as possible when a price increase is in the works. If it is the role of the salesperson to be seen as a strategic asset to the customer, then there must be a level of trust and respect between both parties. If, as the salesperson, you play dumb and don't give the customer any indication a price advance is coming—when in fact you know it is coming—then certainly you are not being respectful or strategic.

The signal can be as simple as letting the customer know there might be a price increase in the future, but without indicating any of the specifics. Certainly the salesperson should not mention anything regarding timing, amount, or the products or services affected. There are two reasons for this approach. First, it allows for last-minute adjustments. Often, when companies develop their pricing strategies, they only establish overall pricing targets in step 1. They then wait until they are as close as possible to the planned date of the increase to determine exactly what the amount will be. There is nothing wrong with this tactic, but it explains why the salesperson should not communicate anything specific early in the process. Second, specific information should not be communicated because the salesperson does not know for sure what the customer may do with the information. If given specific information regarding a price increase, the customer may decide to share it with a competitor as a way of getting a better price. With knowledge of a specific price increase, customers also could decide to alter their buying habits to take advantage of the situation. A significant change in a customer's buying pattern could in turn create other issues for the salesperson and the vendor's overall business plan.

The best way for a salesperson to handle this step is by speaking only in broad terms and by only delivering the information by telephone or in person. The salesperson should not put any information he decides to share about pricing in writing. At this point, putting information in writing will give customers ammunition they could decide to use against the salesperson later on.

The objective of this step is for the salesperson to get a sense for how the customer is going to respond to the increase. I recommend doing this step thirty to forty-five days ahead of the date the salesperson is planning to give the customer information of the specific price increase. The lead time of thirty to forty-five days is only a general number; depending on the industry or order frequency, the lead time may be less or more. Generally speaking, the more frequently the customer orders, the shorter the lead time should be. Conversely, the longer it is between customer orders, the longer the lead time needed to carry out this step.

A customer reacting negatively to the salesperson's comments about a potential price increase doesn't always mean there will be problems actually executing the price increase. This is where the salesperson's knowledge of the customer and key players in the customer's company, as developed in step 5, becomes critical. If the salesperson expects his key contact is going to react negatively to the increase, then it becomes essential for the salesperson to find as many ways as possible to meet with his other contacts within the customer's company.

Step 8: Formalize Expectations and Goals with the Sales Force for Each Customer

The salesperson is now armed not only with the FDPOV, but also with the initial comments the customer may have shared when the salesperson signaled the upcoming price increase. Based on all of the input received and work done so far, the saleperson is now prepared to formalize for each customer what the objective is for the increase. Breaking down the objective by customer gives the salesperson even more input and therefore allows the salesperson to buy into the project even more.

If the objectives developed at the customer level are not as aggressive as they should be, then the sales management team must make adjustments. They can, for instance, break down the objectives between revenue and dates. Sometimes what appears to be missing in achieving an overall revenue goal (i.e., what the price increase will contribute to your top or bottom line) can be made up by changing the dates of when an increase is going to take effect. Another method would be blocking certain order quantities at an old price. There will always be multiple ways to achieve a price increase goal, and before anything is decided, it is essential to review all of the available options.

Step 9: Present the Price Increase to Customers and Gain Their Commitment

Finally, it is time to present the increase to the customer. The most important thing for you, as the salesperson, to remember is not to ask the customer if you can take a price increase. You can't *ask*. They must *tell* the customer what the price increase is and explain any special instructions associated with it.

When salespeople share the news with the customer, they must maintain eye contact with the customer and speak with a firm voice. Professional buyers especially will pick up on any hesitation on the part of the salesperson, and they will use this hesitation against the salesperson. The buyer will immediately push back, knowing the salesperson who hesitates is not comfortable with the price increase. The need for a firm voice is certainly essential if the conversation is taking place over the telephone.

Strong, forceful communication is a must. Preparation should help the salesperson deliver the message with confidence. Knowledge of the customer's critical needs and the FDPOV the salesperson has developed now come into play as well. The salesperson must share with the customer as much information as needed. It's at this point where many customers will say the price increase is unacceptable and they have no other choice but to go with another vendor. This type of response is normal, and a salesperson should not be upset upon hearing it.

For customers to say they are going to switch vendors is one thing, but actually doing it is an entirely different matter. The cost in time and money they would have to go through to switch suppliers likely would be significant. Typically, the cost to convert to a new supplier is much higher than a buyer thinks. If you are the salesperson and you believe the customer may actually incur this problem, then you should make the cost of converting to a different supplier part of your FDPOV. Being so prepared in advance can go a long way in helping you feel confident, and it also gives you another tool you can use with the customer if it becomes necessary.

Step 10: Reinforce the Price Increase by Sharing the FDPOV

After communicating the price increase, the salesperson again should reinforce the FDPOV. Typically, this step is best done in person, on the next sales call, but if the time between calls is too great, then a telephone call would be suitable. Reinforcing the price increase in person gives the salesperson the opportunity to read the customer's reaction and see if there are any other issues that may have to be handled. This, of course, becomes far more difficult over the telephone and is next to impossible to do via an e-mail or letter.

Sharing the FDPOV allows the salesperson to determine exactly how the customer is feeling and if there will be any ramifications in the long term because of the increase. By discussing the FDPOV and tying it to the customer's critical needs, the salesperson has the potential to come away with additional sales opportunities.

Ten Steps to More Profit

The ten-step process works. Numerous companies use it successfully. The single biggest reason it works is because it gets the sales force involved early in the process. Implementing the ten steps can take anywhere from thirty days to six months. Variance is due to the vendor's industry and its financial condition. Typically, the longer the lead time, the better the end results will be. Shorter lead times create more difficulties for everyone. The key to success is in the proper planning by the salesperson and sales management.

CHAPTER 13

Purchasing Departments and the Professional Buyer

A GROUP OF SALESPEOPLE talking about their most difficult customers always makes for an interesting discussion. Salespeople love to share stories about how a particular buyer drives them crazy. As much as salespeople have stories about buyers, the same goes for buyers having stories about salespeople. Get a group of buyers together and they'll share one story after another about various salespeople and the ongoing hassles they have with them.

Yes, there are some very positive buyer and vendor relationships; however, for each positive one, there are probably two or three that are quite poor. Understanding the buyer and, in particular, *professional* buyers and the departments in which they work can be next to impossible. Some buying departments even encourage conflict with the vendors with whom they interact. At the same time, most buying departments want to work with their vendors. They only ask that the vendors do so in a professional manner that respects the buyer's objectives.

Professional buyers go by any number of different names. A few of the more common ones include *procurement officer, purchasing agent, buyer, sourcing manager,* and *supply-chain coordinator.* Their departments also can have a wide range of names including Purchasing, Asset Control, Supply Chain, and Vendor Management. Regardless of the names and titles involved, the objectives remain the same. These employees want to source goods and services from vendors in a manner that allows the employer for whom they work to achieve its overall objectives. For the sake of keeping things simple throughout this chapter, I will refer to these employees as "professional buyers."

Over the years both as a salesperson and now as a consultant, I've had the opportunity to deal with buying departments at both ends of the spectrum. My objective, however, has always remained the same—find a way to do business with them in a way that allows me to make a profit and the buyers to achieve their objectives. If salespeople can enter into every situation with this in mind, they will be more likely to achieve short- and long-term success. The challenge, of course, is in knowing how to do it, because as with anything, it's far easier to say something than it is to actually do it.

Who Is the Professional Buyer?

Professional buyers are exactly that—professionals. These people take their jobs seriously and they should, since their actions can and will impact the overall operations of the organizations they work for. Any salesperson who views the professional buyer as nothing more than a barrier to overcome is going to face difficult issues in the long term. As basic as it might be, I am always amazed at the number of salespeople who still think the professional buyer is an obstacle that must be removed from their path on the way to closing the sale.

Regardless of how buying departments may choose to treat the vendors with whom they deal, it is absolutely essential for the salesperson to treat these buyers with respect. Over the years, I've found very few occasions where a salesperson has been able to achieve success with a professional buying department without showing anything other than the highest level of respect. This does not mean salespeople need to bow down to the purchasing department. It merely means the salespeople should show respect at all times.

More times than not I've watched buying departments change how they interact with a particular vendor based on how the vendor deals with them. The premise is simple. If salespeople want to be treated with respect, they need to treat others with respect. Purchasing departments may initially be tough on any new vendor or salesperson who calls on them. Purchasing departments use this approach because they know it is easier to loosen up their demands of vendors and salespeople *after* a solid relationship has been established than it is to tighten the expectations later.

The New Vendor

Purchasing departments are notorious for demanding that new vendors supply excessive amounts of information before they will even consider the vendor for anything. I share this as advice because if your goal is high-profit selling, then in some circumstances, it's just not worth the time and effort that is necessary to break in a new customer. You need to have keen judgment, because it is not unusual for a buying department to use a potential new vendor as nothing more than a source of information. The information buyers gather from a potential vendor can then be used with their current suppliers to secure better deals. If you want to go through life doing nothing more than serving as an information provider, then go right ahead. If, on the other hand, your goal is to maximize your profit potential, then it only makes sense to focus on customers where the time you invest has the potential of returning a proper level of profit.

The goal of professional buyers isn't to bring chaos and confusion to salespeople. On the contrary, their job is to make things flow as smoothly as possible within their department and company. Many salespeople believe the role of the professional buyer is pretty easy and consists of nothing more than making ever-increasing demands of them. Truth be told, for many professional buyers, the time they spend with salespeople *is* the easiest part of their day. Rarely do salespeople fully comprehend the issues professional buyers go through inside their organizations. Yes, reducing costs can be a key part of a purchasing department's responsibility, but if salespeople think this translates into lower prices for what they sell, then they are missing the whole point. A purchasing department might be charged with lowering costs for their company, but how they do it is up to them. This is where salespeople who have taken the time to develop a relationship with their buyers are going to be at an advantage.

Before we jump into the issue of lowering prices, let's look at other things purchasing departments can do to lower costs. Cost-lowering efforts may involve the following techniques:

1. Decreasing the number of suppliers they work with

2. Reducing the number of items they inventory

3. Reducing the total amount of inventory, thus increasing their turns

4. Changing how they pay invoices

5. Changing payment terms and currencies used

6. Altering how and when inventory is received in their system

7. Altering how they ship individual units

8. Changing the order lead time

9. Bundling products together to benefit shipping/receiving

10. Establishing computer-to-computer data exchange

11. Implementing auto-replenishment ordering systems

12. Using third-party buying groups

13. Trading goods or services with other partners

14. Sourcing through alternative channels or vendors

This list is by no mean inclusive of everything purchasing departments can do, but it does provide an overview of the numerous tools they have at their disposal to help reduce costs. None of the items listed has anything to do with the absolute price of anything, and that's the first point you need to know in understanding how to sell to a buying department. Price is not everything, no matter what the buyer may say.

Your objective as a salesperson is to understand the value of each of these fourteen cost-lowering techniques as employed by the buyer. To start, you need to understand how purchasing departments operate and how their results are measured; then you will be in a position to maximize profit potential and allow your buyers to achieve their objectives.

Understanding How the Buyer Operates

The first step in working with buyers and understanding how they operate begins with taking the time to listen to what they have to say and, more important, showing interest in how they do they job. In my experience, buyers generally are willing to open up with salespeople who truly show a sincere interest in how they do their job. One of the most compelling lines of questioning that works with professional buyers is to ask them to share with you the type of software system they use and to explain their supply-chain process. Because both of these areas are critical to any professional buyer, more often than not, I've found that buyers will discuss openly these areas.

To make the discussion as beneficial as possible, take the time to find out as much as possible about computer systems used by others in the same industry. The same applies to understanding the supply chain. I can't begin to recount the number of warehouses—not only in the United States, but also around the world—that I've had the opportunity to walk through during my sales career. I find the experience of touring warehouses and other supply-chain facilities to be extremely beneficial. The more I tour, the more knowledge I can share with purchasing agents. The more I share with them, the more they in turn share with me. This type of learning is essential, as it has provided me with countless opportunities to show buyers how they can reduce their financials while, at the same time, not lowering the prices they are willing to pay for what I'm selling.

Warehouse Tours and the Buyer

I suggest that anytime you begin calling on a major new account you ask early in the relationship to take a tour of the supply-chain facility. When buyers are taken out of their normal office environment, they tend to open up more. They are getting the opportunity to show off something that makes them proud, and anytime people are proud of something, they will always share more information. When you are touring the supply-chain facility with the buyer or other representative, use the time to ask the customer as many questions as possible. Also, use the tour to explore issues beyond what it is you are selling. Asking questions regarding the overall operations of the facility further demonstrates to the buyer your concern and interest.

Working with a purchasing department is no different from working with a department within your own company, or at least that's how you should view it. Taking this approach reinforces the level of respect and support and helps to ensure that warehouse tours are engaging and beneficial for both you and the buyer. Don't forget that the tour must also be beneficial to the buyer, because you are taking the buyer away from other duties. During the tour, share with the buyer your observations about other warehouse facilities. Ask the buyer questions that will raise awareness of details that normally wouldn't be at the forefront of the buyer's mind. Your goal is to make sure the buyer gains as much out of the tour as you are getting from it.

Learning the Customer's Computer System

Discussions regarding computer systems often open up the same level of dialogue with a buyer that can be gained from a warehouse tour. You need to explore this topic with the buyer and everyone else with whom you come in contact in the purchasing department. Computer systems are either loved or hated by most buyers, so the topic has the potential to generate a lot of discussion. Listen for comments about how information is recorded and the type of reports the buyer can generate from the system. This type of information helps you begin to understand the process the buyer goes through to make decisions. You don't have to press for explanations about the process in detail. Some company policies prohibit buyers from discussing specific evaluation details. The way around this is to piece together enough information by exploring how the computer system operates and how the buyer interacts with it. Salespeople who know how to leverage this kind of information can show buyers how they can meet their objectives without having to reduce any amounts paid to the salesperson.

That being said, though, it never hurts for you to ask specifically how buyers are evaluated in their own job. In interviews I've had as a consultant with many buyers across a wide range of industries, I'm stunned by how few buyers ever get asked this question. It's as if salespeople consider the subject taboo. My view is that there is no subject not worth bringing up with buyers if it has the potential to help them do their job. If you frame your questions regarding how the buyer's own job performance is evaluated in the context of wanting to help the buyer, it will at least allow the buyer to realize the question is being asked in good faith.

My Three Hours with a Buyer

At one point in my sales career I was selling to a large customer who represented a significant portion of my company's business. My attempt at getting information from the buyer never seemed to go anywhere, due to the limited amount of time we had together in the buyer's office. Our meetings were always very professional, but because we had so many topics to cover, I was never able to ask the exploratory questions I knew I needed to ask. My attempts at scheduling additional meeting times were always rejected, with the buyer stating there was no time on the calendar. Finally, I asked the buyer for a tour of his company's main warehouse to help me learn more about how my company could service him better. The request came as a shock to the buyer, and he agreed it would be good to take a tour, as he had not personally toured the warehouse in several years.

The outcome of the tour was eye-opening. I had nearly three hours of one-on-one time with the buyer between traveling to the warehouse, touring it, and having lunch. During this time, the buyer changed into a completely relaxed individual and shared with me critical information about how his company's accounting system operated and the things purchasing had to do every month-end and quarter-end to make its goals. I found myself suddenly with the keys to the company. I now knew what times of the month and quarter were the optimal periods to meet with the buyer. This new information allowed me to change the way I dealt with the customer. In the end, I was able to not only substantially increase the amount of business I did with the customer, but also to experience a dramatic reduction in the number of discussions I had with the buyer over price. Ultimately, these achievements meant more volume and more profit. The final outcome for the customer was that he loved working with my company and me. The buyer felt everything I did fit perfectly into the plans for the purchasing department. To this day, I have no idea if the buyer realized all of the information he shared with me during that three-hour period of our warehouse tour. What matters, though, is how beneficial it was for both the customer and me.

Whenever I share this story with salespeople, I remind them that circumstances may not always allow for a tour of a warehouse. If that's the case, you need to be on the lookout for an event or other opportunity where you can have an extended discussion with the buyer away from the office.

Do Outside Meetings Include Any Risk for You?

There is a downside to the strategy of getting the buyer out of the office. You may share information the buyer can use against you or your company. In extremely competitive industries, many buying departments use this strategy as a way of gaining the upper hand with vendors. Some buyers early in a new relationship are eager and willing to meet a salesperson off-site in a more relaxed setting. New salespeople and veteran salespeople are most susceptible at falling for this ploy, and the results can and will impact the bottom-line profit for months and years to come. New salespeople are vulnerable because they are flattered by the interest and attention they're getting from someone they see as an expert in the industry. Veteran salespeople fall for it only because they don't think anybody would dare use the technique on them to try and get information.

If there is a lesson here it is that salespeople need to maintain their guard at all times. Anytime you go into any type of a meeting with a buyer or anyone else from purchasing, you must come to the meeting with a list of questions. As long as you keep the focus on asking the buyer questions, you run less of a chance of saying something that could come back to hurt the bottom-line profit of your company.

Understanding a Buyer's Objectives

All buyers have objectives. There is nothing new about this observation, but what most salespeople fail to keep in mind is that typically the objectives the buyer is charged with meeting are spread across a wide number of vendors. Too many times, salespeople feel the buyer is attacking them alone. You need to remember that buyers always will choose to make their numbers in the easiest manner possible. There is nothing wrong with that strategy. Why would anyone work harder than he has to? With that in mind, buyers naturally will go after price reductions or other forms of savings from those vendors they know they can successfully secure a better deal from. Sure, this isn't shocking, but it never ceases to amaze me how few salespeople fully grasp the implications of what's going on here. Simply put, the salesperson who is seen as the one least likely to bend on pricing or to make other concessions is going to be the one the buyer is least likely to go after for concessions.

It is so important for you to always remain firm with buyers, even when dealing with minor issues. It's not your objective to annoy the buyer, but it is your objective to show the buyer you will not cave in easily. As long as buyers can reach their objectives in dealing with other vendors, the sales-person who remains firm will not be challenged unnecessarily over price or anything else.

Vendor Letters and Requests

One tactic used by many purchasing departments is to send to all suppliers a letter stating that for any number of different reasons, it is necessary to have every supplier agree to new terms. The new terms might be anything from a percent reduction in list prices to an agreement to extend payment terms by another thirty, sixty, or even ninety days. Letters of this type come in all forms, including e-mail, regular mail, and even overnight delivery. The language may vary but the request is the same. The purchasing department is looking to save money. I have one thing to say to you or anyone else who receives a letter like this—ignore it! I can't say it enough. *Ignore the letter.* The worst thing you can do is respond to it in any manner whatsoever. You should not even acknowledge to the customer that you received the letter. By acknowledging the letter was received, you are admitting you read the letter. By reading the letter, you are admitting you have an opinion as to how to respond, and *that* is the first step in caving into the demands of the customer.

I'm astounded by the number of vendors that do respond to requests of this type and the number of vendors that will, on the merits of the letter itself, agree to a reduction in price. The fact that any vendor caves to this type of request tells me the vendor was already overcharging.

For purchasing departments, sending this type of letter is like printing money. The cost of the actual letter is minimal. It's something an intern or administrative assistant can handle in a few hours. Now, look at what the purchasing department gets in return. It gets free money from any company that agrees to the requested changes. If you doubt this happens, then why do so many purchasing departments send out these types of letters? They certainly would not keep sending these letters if they weren't somewhat productive. I've had many buyers tell me how they routinely send out these types of letters. They will send out letters to a defined list of vendors each quarter, knowing they will earn a certain amount of discounts or savings each time they do it.

As I have already emphasized, if you receive a letter of this type, you should ignore it. Only when you receive a follow-up letter, or are personally asked by your buyer what your response is to the letter, should you respond. The response I tell all salespeople to give is simply, "We already offer you the best price that allows you to maximize your return on investment with us, so there was no reason for us to respond to you." The objective is to be blunt and firm. If you waver in any way when dealing with a request of this type, you will find yourself giving up profit.

Increasing Your Margin on Friday Afternoon

One of the best ways to increase margin is by being in a position to serve the buyer better than other vendors. Rarely will anyone find a buyer who is not overworked trying to keep everyone happy in the organization. The purchasing department tends to not get the respect it deserves in an organization. All this adds up to professional buyers who often find they are racing to get things done, particularly on Friday afternoons. If you are selling a commodity or items that are easily interchanged with other competitive items, then Friday afternoons can be a great time to gain incremental business. On Friday afternoons, buyers often want the path of least resistance. If you call and can help the buyer get things done faster, then you'll win new business, without having your margins squeezed.

There is only one rule to follow: Your phone call has to be about something important. After asking the buyer about a particular item, you now have an open door to ask if there's anything else you can help the buyer with. If you have a reputation with the buyer of being able to deliver on what you promise, then it is possible the buyer will ask you to assist with another issue, such as shipping additional product.

The Friday afternoon strategy also works well at other times—for instance, when you know the buyer is likely entering a busy period and may be stressed or in a state of panic trying to get things completed. I do not recommend this approach if you sell anything other than items that are interchangeable with a competitor's items the customer may already stock. For salespeople who have a unique product offering, calling the buyer at this time may easily wind up creating more downside risk than upside potential.

Buyers work with multiple groups. In fact, in many companies, the purchasing department may interface with more people than anyone else in the company, with the exception of human resources. The challenge a purchasing department has is in keeping all of these groups happy and satisfied. This can become a difficult task when the purchasing department switches suppliers to save money, only to have the employees who are using the product start to complain. For many purchasing departments and buyers, the most difficult part of their job is dealing with the people they are supposed to be serving. Purchasers often have to stock certain items only because of the hassles they would encounter from employees if they switched to another product, even if the switch would save the company money. More than one purchasing manager has shared with me this kind of story. The lesson here for you is to make sure the item the purchasing department is buying is in demand by the end users, then you can leverage this information to your advantage.

(*Note:* The concept of establishing relationships with end users in order to achieve better results in working with a purchasing department is not something I'm going to discuss in this book, only because the concept is basic selling. Let's just say this concept is essential for grasping many of the other concepts described in this book.)

Working with purchasing departments is not something you should avoid or view as being a significant hurdle in closing sales. Think of the purchasing department as an extension of yourself. Always remember that as much as they are buyers, they also are sellers. They have to spend a significant amount of time "selling" what they've purchased to their internal customers. Additionally, the purchasing department is often one of the first departments that corporate management will call upon when the company needs to reduce costs. When you have done your job and made the effort to understand how the purchasing department works and what the department's objectives are, then you will be in the best position to help the buyer.

RFPs and RFQs: The Bidding Process

WHETHER IT'S A REQUEST for proposal (RFP), request for quotation (RFQ), or one of the other methods companies use to ask vendors to submit a proposal, the challenge for the seller can be daunting. Nearly every salesperson has had to deal with an RFP or similar process. These documents can be as simple as a single-page letter or as complex as a 200-page report requiring input from multiple partners.

For many salespeople, responding to an RFP is more painful than writing even the most difficult college term paper. The amount of time it takes to complete an RFP can easily consume many days of precious time. As painful as it is to respond to an RFP, waiting for a response can be even harder. Even if the answer is "yes" and the sale happens, it may not quite live up to initial expectations. Obviously, the emotion, time, and resources it takes to deal with an RFP can, in the end, take a major toll on any salesperson or sales team. For this reason, I'm a firm believer that salespeople should ignore the majority of RFPs they receive. The time and effort is simply not worth it. Most RFPs are written with a predetermined outcome in mind.

It is not uncommon for a specific vendor to assist the company or purchasing department with writing the RFP. This vendor almost guarantees the RFP is written in a way that will ensure that it gets the business. About the only place where there are legal restrictions on this practice is when the RFP is from a government entity. For the vast majority of bids, though, there is bias involved. Even if there is a perception that every vendor has a fair opportunity to win a bid, the reality is that the person or group making the final decision typically has criteria that are going to favor a vendor they already knew they wanted to select. Then the RFP process becomes nothing more than a mere formality.

Are RFPs a Good Use of Your Time?

Salespeople always ask me if it is possible to maximize profit when the vendor is being selected through a bidding process. My answer is that it is very difficult to maximize profit if you are the company that "wins" the bid. However, that doesn't mean it is not a good practice to respond to a bid. I believe it can be smart to respond to an RFP or other bid if you have a clearly defined strategy. This chapter explains how to determine if it even makes sense to respond to a bid and how to develop a strategy to maximize the time and effort you spend on the process.

Sometime back I was asked by managers at another company to partner with them on a major project for a customer that was a large global company. The potential for both my company and the other company was significant. We were entering the process late, having been asked by the customer to submit a proposal in less than a week. Normally a proposal of this type would take several weeks to prepare; however, we decided it was worth doing since the payout was so large.

We quickly found ourselves racing against the clock to submit what we felt was a first-class proposal that would win the business for us. Both my company and the partner company were pleased with the information we provided. After we submitted the plan, we all felt we would surely be receiving a phone call from the customer, congratulating us on our superior plan. Needless to say, we never got the project. The only thing we received was the rejection e-mail. I believe the customer was already leaning toward a different vendor, but requested other vendors to submit bids as a way of quickly gathering free information. The information we and the other suppliers gave the customer was then used to secure a better deal with the vendor ultimately selected. In the end, we wasted our time. Looking back on the bid package, we were foolish to even think we might be able to earn the business. The sole reason we put the bid package together was because the opportunity was so large. That right there is one of the biggest mistakes salespeople make when deciding to respond to a bid. They respond using the excuse that the opportunity is too big to pass up. I call it the "lottery ticket syndrome." I know of a lot of people who won't buy lottery tickets because they believe the odds are stacked against them. However, as soon as the jackpot reaches record levels, they jump in and buy tickets. They buy tickets believing the prize is simply too big and can't be ignored. If they don't think the odds are in their favor when the prize is small, what makes them believe the odds will be in their favor when the prize is large? The odds aren't any better. In fact, they are much worse because of the increased number of people playing the lottery when the pot is so high.

Benefits of the Small RFP

The same applies to RFPs. If the size of the bid to be awarded is seen as large, the number of vendors that submit proposals can be equally large. This is why oftentimes when I'm working with companies, I tell them to focus their attention on the smaller bids. Focusing on smaller bids typically means there is less competition and, therefore, the profit potential as a percent of total revenue can be larger. As simple as this concept is, I'm amazed at the number of companies and salespeople who disregard it. They would rather spend significant time submitting proposals for projects that are "too big to ignore." Remember, the title of this book is *High-Profit Selling*. Don't lose sight of what that title means. High-profit selling is not only about being able to sell your products and services at a full price, but also about being able to do so in an effective manner. When I say being *effective,* I mean embracing a sales process that does not waste time.

Writing the RFP Gives You the Upper Hand

"If you didn't write the RFP, your competitor did." I like this phrase. It is something all salespeople need to keep in mind when first determining if they should even respond to an RFP or similar bid. Many times the customer already has a vendor in mind when it releases a bid. If the goal is to maximize profit with a customer who does business through bids, then naturally your objective is to be the one who gets to help write the RFP. And if you've followed all the advice as recommended in the preceding chapters, you will be in a much better position than most salespeople to be able to help write the RFP or bidding document.

When you are able to at least influence what goes into an RFP, you have the ability to ensure that what you do best is included among the performance requirements. I am not advocating you should work to make the bid document so one-sided that the customer is not getting what it needs out of it. Not only is that bad business, it also is unethical. What I do encourage is that you make sure the document highlights the customer's critical needs. Then, if you have done your homework with the customer, you will understand better than any other vendor how to deal with the customer's critical needs.

Use the chance to help write the RFP to demonstrate your strategic skills to the customer. That way, not only are you helping to structure the RFP to ensure your odds of earning the business, but you also are positioning yourself for a potentially expanded role, where the customer can tap you as a knowledge expert.

Step 1: Determine Your Strategy

For the majority of bid proposals where you have not been able to help write the RFP, the first decision that must be made is whether it is even worth responding to. There are four possible reasons you would choose to respond to an RFP:

1. To earn the business by winning the contract
2. To earn the business, but with a modified contract or plan
3. To lose the bidding process, with the goal of being a strong No. 2
4. To lose, but learn key information or send a signal

Let me briefly explain each one of these strategies, and then I will share in depth how each one works.

Earn the Business by Winning the Contract

This strategy is self-explanatory, as it says the goal is to get the business following the guidelines laid out in the bid package.

Earn the Business, with a Modified Contract or Plan

This is not a strategy that you can use often if bidding on a government or public contract. However, with other RFPs, a customer may become overwhelmed by the number of proposals received and start revising its expectations. This occurs frequently with customers who are releasing a bid package for a business contract or project they have not undertaken before.

Lose the Bidding Process with the Goal of Being a Strong No. 2

This can be a highly effective strategy, especially for government or public contracts where prices get beat down to a point where the winning supplier is making very little profit. The beauty of this strategy is that by coming in second, you are in a position to provide all of the last-minute work the company that won the contract is not able to provide. By helping the customer at the last minute, you can typically make a higher margin than the company that won the bid is able to charge.

Lose, but Learn Key Information or Send a Signal

This is an excellent strategy to use when first starting to work with a new customer. It acknowledges that the chances of earning the business are quite low on this initial bid, but the information you can learn will open doors with the customer in the long term. This approach also can be used to send a signal that, as a vendor, you intend to be seen as a potential supplier. It also is a great way to learn what other competitors are doing from a pricing standpoint.

Determining which one of these four options to use as the foundation for your response is critical. Failure to determine a strategy before starting on the proposal will result in too many last-minute changes to the document that gets submitted. Understanding the strategy before starting also allows you to decide how much time and resources to allocate toward developing the response.

Let's now dig deeper into each one of the four strategies.

1. *If the goal is to earn the business or contract, then structure the proposal to win.* On the surface this advice sounds simple, but executing this strategy properly means guidelines have to be set as to what you actually say in the contract. If guidelines aren't established before starting to write the response, there can be what I refer to as "giveaway creep." Some salespeople have the habit of putting additional things into a proposal at the last minute. Salespeople love to do this because they suddenly begin to think of all of the work they've done developing the response, and they want to add "one more thing" to ensure they win the business. The problem is that there are too many "one more things" that can get added to a contract. Ultimately, the proposal won't allow these salespeople to make the profit they need to make.

2. *Strategize to earn the business, but also try to influence the customer to modify its contract or plan.* This option can work very well in nongovernment or public situations. The challenge is to determine up-front if the customer releasing the

bid is most likely going to have to revise its expectations. If you have previous knowledge of the customer, then you may be able to make this determination by reading the RFP and looking for possible gray areas. For example, the contract is asking for certain items but not asking for other items; that may indicate that the customer has not thoroughly thought about its needs. If you decide that the customer will most likely have to modify the contract before implementing it, then the information you initially provide does not need to be firm.

In these types of situations, you can focus on asking questions and providing information to customers that gets them thinking about what they should be requesting. Your goal is to present the customer with enough information to compel them to arrange a meeting with you to discuss the matter further. By having a meeting with the customer early in the bidding process, you can influence the customer to begin thinking about what may need to be changed in the RFP before selecting a vendor.

Using this approach can be risky; however, for those salespeople who otherwise would not be able to generate a proposal that delivers them adequate profit, this approach can be the best option. The benefit is in the discussions you are able to have with the customer. These discussions can help the customer view you as a knowledge expert who can lend strategic advice on other matters of interest. When this occurs, you may be in a position to provide the customer with a much wider assortment of products or services than either of you initially expected.

3. Strategize to lose the bidding process, especially if there's intense pricing pressure, but set the goal of being a strong No. 2 supplier. Too many bids end with one company earning the business, but at a price that eliminates any room for error on the profit that company can expect to make. Numerous times I've received calls from companies asking for assistance in helping work through contracts that begin to fall apart because the intense bidding drove the price down too low. These situations may initially give the customer a very strong sense of satisfaction; however, in the end the customer and the vendor both lose because of the low-profit margins.

For example, the vendor that won the contract may find itself under such intense pricing pressure that it is not in a position to deal with any changes or even fulfill all of the terms of the contract. When this occurs, the customer may be forced to source a product or service from another supplier. The vendor that came in second in the bidding process often is the one the customer turns to first for assistance. The second-place vendor is now in a position to demonstrate what it can do. Best of all, this vendor can typically provide the product or service at a much higher level of profit than the vendor that won the contract is earning.

Usually, this strategy can succeed only after you do some initial work. Salespeople often can find out some competitive information that leads them to realize the profit margins are going to be squeezed too low to be meaningful. In some situations, you can make this determination based on the history of the customer and how it has handled contracts in the past. Typically a customer that beats up vendors to maximize a low price on one contract will come back and follow the same strategy on the next contract. Knowing this type of information can guide you in determining how to respond.

When a customer tries to get a heavily reduced price, it is not unusual for the vendor that came in second to become a secondary supplier for the customer. The company that won the contract gets significantly more business, but receives a lower profit margin in terms of percent. On the other hand, the vendor that took second place does far less total business but at a much higher profit margin.

4. *Strategize to lose the bidding process, but with the goal of learning key information or sending a signal.* When I first explain this strategy to companies, I'm often met with blank stares. People wonder, Why would anyone go through the work of completing a bid package to deliberately lose? It may seem like an illogical move, but in the long run it can be one of the smartest decisions you can make. Let's first look at the idea of learning key information. If you have very little experience in working with the customer releasing the bid package, it is unlikely you will win the bid. It only makes sense, then, for you to focus your efforts on learning as much as possible, so you are in a better position to earn the next bid.

Another excellent reason to use this approach is the increased possibility that you may secure more meetings with the customer because of your participation in the bid process. I've worked with many a company on a bid package for the sole purpose of developing as many relationships as possible with the customer. The bidding process can create an environment conducive to developing relationships. In these situations, it becomes possible for the vendor not only to gain key new information, but also to promote itself as a subject matter expert.

The challenge with this strategy is that the customer has to be someone you know will continue to generate business in the months and years following the current bid package. The more additional selling opportunities the customer presents, the more promising this strategy can be. This strategy can even work with those customers who release bid packages with the stipulation that there can be no contact with the customer. If the objective is not to win the bid, then there is no penalty for attempting to have meetings with the customer about the bid package. Minimally, by participating in a bid package of this type, the salesperson sometimes discovers the opportunity for meetings after the company has completed the bid process.

The bidding process can be a way for you to communicate your expectations. By submitting a price that will knowingly not win, you are telling the customer that you are not a low-price provider. You are sending a signal. This strategy can help minimize future discussions with the customer over price issues, because the customer will know that low price is not an option with you.

For those bid packages where everyone who submits a proposal will have the pricing information made public, this strategy can be used to advertise what you will or won't do. Although it may seem counterproductive, there is no loss in this strategy; in fact, it can go a long way in helping you create your niche in the marketplace. Allowing competitors and customers to see who offered what pricing can help customers and vendors make better long-term decisions about who they want to partner with. What this does is allow you to use your selling time more effectively, because customers will have a clearer understanding of what you will or won't accept with regard to pricing.

Step 2: Develop Your Minimum/Maximum Standards

Once you have determined the overall strategy, the next step is to determine the minimum and maximum standards for what will be put into the bid package. The minimum and maximum standards consist of not only the pricing, but also the services that may need to be included in the bid package. Determining these parameters before starting to work on the bid helps prevent the last-minute proposal hedging to which many salespeople fall victim. Proposal hedging (or "giveaway creep") is the tendency many salespeople have to suddenly offer the customer one more thing as a way to make the offer more enticing. The problem is that the items offered tend to be more to satisfy the sensibilities of the salesperson rather than the needs of the customer.

Select a Price Range

To help maintain a high level of profit from the deal, you must determine the range of prices to present to the customer. During the bidding process, it is not necessary to finalize the price, but only to establish a range—and to back up the range with data. If the pricing range selected is not backed up with data, it becomes meaningless. Almost without exception, the price ultimately offered to the customer will be the lowest price in the range. The data supporting the range needs to include the following:

- Profit the company expects to make

- The value of what the customer will experience in the offering

- Marketplace expectations of what others might bid

- Identification of any variables that might impact the profit over the life of the bid and/or contract

Having data to support each of these criteria will help ensure the bid price offered is both affordable and in line with what your company needs to receive.

Establish Service Parameters

It is equally important to identify at the start of the process any additional services such as additional quality control steps, or more delivery options that you may want to offer the customer. Rather than simply listing these additional services, you must reveal what they cost.

When you are trying to determine which services should even be shown to the customer, keep in mind that services can dramatically reduce the overall profitability of the transaction. Often, the profit a company expects to make from a customer is lost either because the customer demands additional services or the salesperson offers them to the customer. Be careful not to offer items or services that may not be deliverable over the life of the proposed contract.

Once you have determined all of these variables, the results should be communicated to everyone who may be involved in developing the bid package. This extra effort does two things. First, it prevents people from putting things they shouldn't into bid packages. Second, it helps hold people accountable. By letting everyone see what can and cannot be offered, the vendor's employees will be able to hold each other accountable.

Step 3: Develop Your Options

The third step is to develop a list of the things that could be offered to the customer that the customer would perceive as important but that wouldn't cost you too much. Examples might include your ability to deliver shipments five days per week to a specified location. If you have trucks already in the area, it would be a minimal cost to your company. However, for the customer, it could be a huge way to minimize inventory. For another customer it might be a very specific type of quality control process you can provide for very little cost, but that the customer will see as very important.

The bigger the list of options you can develop, the better—especially if the objective of the bid package is to be able to negotiate a significantly different deal than the customer originally wanted. By developing this list well in advance, you help ensure that regardless of the direction the process goes, there are viable options.

Step 4: Gain Information from the Customer and Others

The more information you can gather prior to developing a response to an RFP, the better. I encourage all salespeople immediately upon receiving an RFP or bid package to contact the customer and have a live conversation. The more opportunities you have to discuss with customers what they want and need, the greater likelihood of success, no matter what strategy you use.

As important as it is to have a meeting with the customer when the bid package is released, it's even better if you can have as many meetings as possible *before* the release of the RFP or bid package. Yes, this step is predicated on your having a relationship with the customer, but you are going to be hardpressed to maximize the profit potential on any bid package without having a good relationship with the customer.

One downside to gathering information is that it is possible to become too focused on bad information. I mean information that is really just a rumor or, worse yet, false information. On large bid projects, it is not unusual for many companies to respond. In so doing, they are asking for information from other suppliers or contractors. These other suppliers who are asked to provide information can either intentionally or accidentally spread false information or start a rumor. Information gathered is not usable information until it can be validated by another source. This is especially true when receiving information about how a competitor might respond to the RFP. If you don't take the time to validate information through a second source, it can become far too easy to give away profit by offering a price that is lower than necessary.

Step 5: Respond and Get the Meeting

Before responding to any RFP or bid, and before going through the effort of presenting the information in a particular format, it is essential to know how the winning vendor is going to be selected. Many government agency bids are done by sealed bid. In this case, the objective is to submit the plan most likely to achieve one of the strategies I discussed in the previous section.

With most bid packages, there is typically what I refer to as a "bake-off," a meeting the customer sets up with the top two or three vendors who have submitted the best packages according to the customer's criteria. When the customer has a bake-off, it is allowing its top picks to come and present their package. These meetings are designed to facilitate a large amount of discussion, and because of their importance, they need to be viewed as the most critical part of the bid process.

Follow-up meetings with the customer allow you to alter how you choose to deliver the initial bid package to the customer. When you learn that the customer is planning follow-up meetings, your objective is not necessarily to win the bid outright, but rather to make sure you are one of the vendors the customer invites for a meeting. If the goal is to be one of the companies selected to meet with the customer, the initial bid package should contain as many questions as possible to stimulate the customer's thinking. Even if the bid package does not ask for questions, you should still provide them.

By including questions in the bid package, you will have a greater likelihood of ensuring the customer will want to meet with you. The questions do not even have to be ones to which you have an answer. In fact, the best questions are many times those to which neither side has the answer. These questions are often so thought-provoking that they beg both sides to discuss them further.

Bake-off meetings are an opportunity for you to not just present the bid package, but more important, to pose questions of your customers to get them thinking in depth about their needs. You want to get customers thinking about issues they otherwise would not have considered. You need to see this meeting as the single best chance to equip customers to see things they previously had not considered. High-profit selling is all about working to create new opportunities and allowing customers to see you as a strategic partner they can't live without.

Using the meeting to put as many questions on the table as possible allows you to not only build additional discussion, but also to uncover many new areas of information. It is vital that you focus the questions on the customer's larger goals and industry, not just the bid package itself. The measurement of a successful meeting is when the customer asks you for another meeting to continue the discussion. Then you are in a position to not only earn the current bid package, but also to receive additional opportunities to do business.

The Value of a Follow-Up Meeting

Regardless of the outcome, you need to always have a follow-up meeting with the customer. Too often, salespeople who do not win a bid simply walk away and move on to the next deal. In doing so, they may be walking away from the chance to learn valuable information from a customer. I personally know of situations where salespeople who lost a bid had a follow-up meeting with the customer to discuss why they did not receive the bid, only to then have the customer give them so much information of value that they were able to successfully secure the next bid.

Bid Selection Renegotiation

Many times, just as a customer is ready to select a vendor, the customer will suddenly ask for a few quick changes. Salespeople get caught in this trap too often. The excitement of winning a large bid clouds the salesperson's judgment, and sharp customers know they can leverage it to their advantage. It's in this final stage that profit can disappear faster than at any other time in the sales process. To avoid this happening to you, you must remain firm when you are face-to-face with the customer and tell the customer that you are not allowed to make any changes to the bid package without first speaking to your office. Holding firm usually will get customers to soften their request. The worst thing you can do is to agree to some minor change, because this response tells the customer the door is open for even more changes.

Sharp customers who use the bidding process for much of their business are notorious for using this last-minute process to secure additional concessions from the vendor. I've had customers share with me how they can significantly improve a contract even after they've selected a vendor by merely making a number of last-minute requests. The salesperson who falls for this strategy is not only giving up profit in the short term, but also is giving up profit that will never be recovered.

Use the bid or RFP process as a great opportunity to build relationships with the customer on as many levels as possible. The more these relationships can be leveraged, both during and after the bid process, the more potential there will be for you to generate higher profits.

15

Position Yourself to Continue Earning High Profits

*T*OP PERFORMER. PRESIDENT'S CLUB. *Gold Circle. Salesperson of the Year.* Nearly all companies have some sort of recognition program to reward what they consider superior performance. To the salespeople who have achieved these levels of recognition, I say, "Job well done." For those salespeople who have yet to achieve the level of recognition and reward they know they are capable of earning, I say, "Don't give up, and every day seek to be the best."

Receiving an award is great, and I'm a firm believer in recognizing performance that goes beyond expectations. Where problems arise is when we attempt to determine what is "beyond expectations." Top-performing salespeople—and by this I mean salespeople who are consistently maximizing the profit they earn for the company—are people who love recognition and reward, but do not rely on it to motivate themselves. I've watched too many salespeople strive to earn the top spot among their peers, only to find another salesperson snatch the award from them at the last minute because of another significant accomplishment. The ensuing letdown can be dramatic and result in less-than-optimal performance for anywhere from a few weeks to several months. If salespeople want to position themselves to consistently earn high profits and high compensation, they have to be prepared to practice self-motivation. At its core, self-motivation is all about how we view ourselves and how we respond to each day's activities.

The sales profession is vital to the success of any economy. Salespeople help both their company and their customers to succeed. For us to help the customer succeed, we have to succeed ourselves. One of my essential beliefs is that salespeople must continually improve their sales skills. This means always monitoring not only sales results, but also sales processes. As salespeople, we must continually improve those sales processes. If we fail to continue to upgrade our selling skills, then we put ourselves in the same boat as any number of industries we've seen fade away over the years. These industries disappeared because the products or services they provided were no longer in demand by the customer, or someone else found a way to make a similar item a little bit better. The same can be said with our selling skills. Too many salespeople who were at one time incredibly successful now find themselves achieving results they are ashamed of. Instead of blaming their inability to sell on their own failure to improve their selling skills, they blame the poor results on the customer's unwillingness to buy.

One Percent Continuous Improvement Process

One of the things I enjoy most about my job is that I'm able to meet thousands of salespeople each year and exchange ideas about what it takes to succeed in sales. The top performers I've met have one trait in common: They believe in their own perfect process. They claim their process in the best one because of the results they've achieved. And in every top performer's process is a continual desire to improve—to find that one idea, no matter how big or small, that can increase the salesperson's success. Out of all of this, I've developed what I call the one percent Continuous Improvement Process (CIP).

The way the one percent CIP works is very simple. Each week you try to improve your sales performance by one percent. Anything improved by one percent each week will result in significant improvement over time. If you understand the power of compounding, you'll see that one percent each week can create significant growth in just one year. To save you the time of figuring it out, I've run the math for you. If you take a baseline of 100 and have it grow by one percent each week for fifty-two weeks, what began as 100 is now 167.77. Let's put that number into context. What salesperson wouldn't like increasing his sales performance by 167 percent in one year? The problem is most salespeople do not believe they can do that. The truth is they *can't*—not if they are trying to do it all in one area. If you are able to find one area where you could improve your performance and see a gain of 167 percent in a year, then you should certainly do it. However, for sales-people who are already high-level performers, the probability of changing one item and seeing such positive results is not very likely. That's why I believe in using the one percent CIP each and every week.

Small Changes Equal Big Improvement

If you are still confused about how this concept works, think of it this way: If you break down what you did last week into 100 separate activities, could you find one that you could improve? I'm sure you could, and that's what the one percent CIP technique is all about—finding a way to improve your sales process by only one percent each week. The compound-ing power of improvement then takes hold when you do this one activity each week. If you are still wondering how or what you can do, begin to take a look at all of the sales activities you did last week. There was probably the opportunity for you to make a couple more phone calls. Maybe there was the opportunity to ask a better question, or possibly you could have stopped checking websites you visit regularly and use that time instead to do something more productive. You see, it's not that difficult to find ways to make yourself more pro-ductive as a salesperson. You could put the one percent CIP technique to work for you right now by using one of the many sales ideas presented in this book and then repeating the process each week.

Improving your sales process is not necessarily going to translate into an equal improvement in your sales results. I've also heard from many salespeople who have used the one percent CIP technique for a year and increased their sales by 20 percent, which represents a significant increase in their compensation. This is what separates top performers from average performers. Top performers will do whatever it takes to succeed. Average performers, on the other hand, are far less inclined to make an investment in something unless they are assured they are going to get the return on investment they want. Now let me ask you a question. Do you want to be an average performer or do you want to be a top performer? I doubt there are many people reading this book who will say they merely want to be an average performer. An average performer is not going to take the time to read this book.

Begin to ask yourself what you can do to improve your sales performance by one percent each week. If you are looking for ideas, visit my website at www.TheSalesHunter.com. It is full of sales tips you can read, listen to on audio, or watch on video. They are all there to help you put into practice the one percent CIP technique.

Your Windshield Is Talking to You

Early in my career, my sales territory encompassed eastern Oregon. If you aren't familiar with eastern Oregon, take a look at a map. It's a massive area with very few people. Without a doubt, it's one of those areas of the United States where cattle outnumber humans by at least ten to one. It's an area where I could find myself driving for 100 miles between sales calls. It's where I first learned that your windshield can talk back to you. In fact, not only does it talk back to you, but it also will process information and develop complex ideas. I'm sharing this story with you because although you may not have sold in an area as deserted as eastern Oregon, you probably have found yourself talking to yourself on occasion.

I remember one afternoon where I was looking at nearly an hour's drive on a barren two-lane road, and as I drove along, with nothing but prairie grass and an occasional herd of cattle in sight, I continued to replay in my mind the disaster of a sales call I had just made. The call was nowhere close to what I had expected it to be, and it was mostly because of mistakes I had made. The more I drove, the more down I was feeling, and the more I was not looking forward to having to make still another sales call. I feared that the disaster of the last call would repeat itself on the next call. The more I thought about what had occurred, the more my windshield talked back to me and the more upset I became. What happened the rest of the day could be viewed as nothing more than going through the motions. I don't remember much about the next call or any of my other calls that day, other than the results were anything but what was expected of me as a sales representative for a major corporation.

I'm sharing this story because I'm sure you can think of similar disastrous sales calls and wasted days. I could easily write a book on all of the disasters I've had and, worse yet, the number of days wasted because of one sales call that went bad and my allowing it to play with my mind. The windshield talking back to me was destroying my sales motivation.

Recovering from the Bad Sales Call

Think for a few minutes about how you responded to a sales call that was a disaster. How long did it take you to recover? How productive were you the rest of the day? Many salespeople, when they have a bad call, go through a "disaster recovery process." The first thing they usually do is make a phone call to their spouse, significant other, or even to their mom. I hate this approach. It's not that I don't like your mom; she is probably a wonderful person. However, what happens is that whoever you call gives you sympathy and comfort and then tells you how everything is going to be just fine and not to worry about it. Excuse me, but I am worrying about it, because when you engage yourself in a sympathy call, it doesn't do enough to get you back at the top of your game. If you are going to be a high performer, you need to be able to use every day and every hour as effectively as you can, and that means being able to bounce back from a failed sales call. High performers have disastrous sales calls, but they differ from mediocre salespeople in what they do after a failed sales call.

The best way to recover from a failed sales call is to immediately call your favorite customer. Your favorite customer will be happy to hear from you and gladly spend a couple minutes on the phone talking about what you sell and how happy the customer is with your product or service and the support you provide. As you can see, it is not as complex as you might think. Call your favorite customer, and after you talk to that person, you'll know again why it is you do what you do. You'll be in a much better position to move forward productively.

Your company is not paying you to call someone for sympathy. Your company expects you to sell, and that is the number one reason I believe the worst thing you can do is to call your significant other or your mother or anyone else who will sympathize with you. Hopefully, you won't find yourself calling your favorite customer every day to help you recover from a bad sales call. First off, the customer is going to start wondering what's wrong with you. Second, if you are having bad sales calls every day, maybe you should look at switching careers. If you are reading this book, though, I am certain you are much closer to the high performer than the one who is struggling.

Always Be Learning

If I were to ask you what you learned yesterday and how you will apply today what you learned, what would you say? A key trait of the high-performing salesperson is the ability to always be learning. If you are intent on putting into practice the one percent CIP technique, you'll always be intent on trying to find as many ways as possible to improve your selling skills. One process that has tremendous potential is asking yourself at the end of each day what you learned that day and how you can use it tomorrow. What you learn might be a particular piece of information you've been trying to discover regarding a specific customer. It could be a new lead or a new benefit you heard from a customer regarding what you sell. The objective is simply to learn something, and then determine how you can use that knowledge tomorrow. I'm serious.

I don't mean "tomorrow" as in some future date, I mean the very next day, because if you do not use vital information quickly, you easily can lose it and never use it. Knowledge not used is wasted knowledge.

So far, we've been talking about how to make the most of each day. Now let's open it up a little bit more and discuss how you can better leverage your weekly activities. If you are going to maximize the amount of profit you can get on each sale, you have to be ready to respond to any situation whenever it occurs. I've shared in other chapters the value and importance of prospecting during holiday weeks and other time periods that most people would consider the worst time to prospect. I've told you how to deal with a sales call that does not go well and how to bounce back faster.

Strategically Planning Your Week

Let's talk about what I believe is one of the most important times of the salesperson's week—Sunday night. Using Sunday night to your advantage in getting ready for the week is the only way you'll ever become a top performer. (For those of you who don't have a typical Monday-through-Friday work routine, don't ignore what I'm about to say. You merely need to move the day to whatever evening is the evening before you start your workweek.)

Sunday night is your pregame meeting with yourself. This is the time for you to make sure you are physically and mentally ready to hit the ground running, hard and fast, Monday morning. Salespeople who wait until Monday mornings to get organized for the workweek are simply not going to be as productive. Yes, I know some of you are thinking that Monday is the worst time to prospect. I agree it's not a good time to prospect, but it is a great time to follow up with existing customers and do other high-value sales activities.

I first came across the idea of leveraging Sunday nights from Lee Iacocca, the CEO who saved Chrysler in the 1980s, and from Jack Welch, the legendary retired CEO of GE. Both of these leaders (who also saw themselves as salespeople in their jobs) would use Sunday evenings to prepare for the week ahead. Their belief was if they wanted to beat the competition, they needed to be ahead of the competition. I like to use Sunday evenings to strategically plan my week and to review my goals and determine what steps I'm going to take to accomplishing them. Notice I didn't say "to build a to-do list." That's the worst thing you can do, because then you've relegated yourself to merely reacting to things. I'd much rather spend my time acting on opportunities. Does that mean you should disregard the reports you need to write and the meetings you need to attend? No. But you do need to make sure these tasks are performed in the context of helping you achieve your goals.

If you are going to use Sunday nights efficiently to help you get off to a fast start in the week ahead, then you also have to learn to use Friday evenings effectively. I believe you need to step away from your job to get needed rest and spend quality time with your family. If you don't learn how to disengage from work on Fridays, you'll never be able to fully use the weekend for doing what you want to do.

Before you start to disengage from work for the weekend, take a few minutes Friday evening to think back on your week and the things that went well. Your objective is to review your week to determine what single activity was your best moment of the week. One week it might be a big sale you closed. Another week the highlight might be as small as merely being able to get somebody's contact information you've been working hard to get. It doesn't matter how big or small—it's all about singling out the biggest thing you accomplished in the week that just ended. Take a couple of minutes to congratulate yourself and savor the success of the week. By focusing on your biggest accomplishment for the past week, you'll be much more inclined to enter the weekend in a positive mood, so you are able to relax and enjoy your weekend more.

Setting Weekly Goals to Build Off Your Successes

While you're savoring your success, also take a couple of minutes to think about what your goal is going to be for the next week. I love this approach, because I'm much more apt to push myself when I'm already feeling good. Don't get carried away with your goal for the upcoming week, as it must be a goal that fits into your overall quarterly and annual goals. The worst thing you can do is to set a completely disjointed new goal just for the sake of doing it. Now, here's the trick—don't make your goal so big you can't achieve it. The weekly goal is not designed to break performance records. It's designed to help you build on your momentum and continue working toward your big goals.

Here's my rule: *Aim for 80 percent chance of success.* The weekly goals I set for myself are goals I have at least an 80 percent chance of achieving. If you think that's pretty basic, you're right. But it accomplishes what I want, which is to enter each week with a positive feeling about the success I had the week before and the success I expect to have with my upcoming weekly goal. That's how I'm able to maintain my momentum. Never underestimate the power of momentum in sales. It is not unusual for a salesperson who has been in a sales slump to finally make that one sale and then get on a roll of closing sale after sale. This momentum can greatly impact your sales motivation and psychology. Setting your goal to where you can most likely achieve it allows you to do just that—*achieve it*. By achieving the weekly goal you've set for yourself, you've increased your momentum, built up your sales motivation, and moved yourself one step closer to achieving your bigger goals.

There's one more piece to the puzzle of using your weekend time effectively. No matter who you are and no matter how much you might say you disconnect from your job on the weekends, there's still a part of your mind that stays engaged with your job. That's why this next step is so important. When you find your mind drifting back to your sales job, let your mind wander to come up with some new ideas. It doesn't matter if the ideas are strategic or tactical—just go ahead and come up with them. Often our best ideas come to us when we've taken a step back from our job.

In my role as a speaker and consultant, I'm fortunate to travel extensively around the world speaking at various conferences and working with a number of salespeople and companies. The amount of time I spend on an airplane and in distant cities affords me an opportunity to brainstorm new ideas that I wouldn't be able to generate if I was buried in my job. This is the beautiful thing about the weekend, too. It gives us a chance to relax and step away from our job and still be able to use the time to help us in our job.

Recording Your Goals and Accomplishments

As I've laid out in the previous sections, weekly goal setting breaks down into three parts:

> Friday evening: Congratulating your success and setting the new goal
>
> Saturday and Sunday: Brainstorming as your mind wanders
>
> Sunday evening: Thinking strategically about how you are going to use the week ahead

Certainly all activities are unique and beneficial, but I think Friday evening has the potential to be particularly helpful in your sales career. Salespeople—regardless of whether they are top performers, average performers, or low performers—routinely tell me that they get a pit in their stomach on Sunday evening as they start thinking about Monday. The reasons they give me are wide-ranging, but the feeling is the same. It is the feeling of not wanting the weekend to end and having to face the issues of the upcoming week. That's why I strongly believe in taking time to celebrate your success on Friday evening and allowing it to sink into your mindset. Then, come Sunday night, you can sit down with two documents in front of you—your goals for the new week, broken down step-by-step, and your successes thus far—so you will be better equipped to take your strategic ideas and use them to achieve your sales goals.

I want to encourage you to not only celebrate your biggest weekly successes, but also to record them in a notebook that you can regularly return to, as an ongoing resource, to generate more ideas. With your goal and success documents in front of you, you can begin strategically assessing how and what you want to do in the upcoming week. Look for ways to break your ideas into smaller ideas that you will be able to leverage as small blocks of time open up in the week to come.

It is absolutely essential to identify specifically what you intend to do once Monday morning rolls around. The things you do must be of high value. If you can start Monday morning fast out of the gate, it's going to make your entire week that much more productive. Plus, you'll have a jump on your competitors, because more than likely, they are going to spend Monday morning wasting time checking e-mail, organizing files, and doing other low-value activities. Yes, "checking e-mail" is a low-value activity and something you can do Sunday evening so that first thing Monday, you are not distracted by the nervous sense you need to check your in-box.

Furthering Your Knowledge and Expertise

Now that I've described several ways you can leverage your time to improve your selling process, I would be remiss if I didn't take a moment to also say that those at the top of the sales world are continuous learners as well. They are always seeking out new information and new ideas. Do you faithfully take one hour a week to expand your sales knowledge base? I'm talking about digging in and discovering new concepts or concepts you may have forgotten. I'm talking about being a disciplined advocate of personal growth. If you have not done so already, check my website (www.TheSalesHunter.com) and start reading the numerous articles and e-books available. You can also access my YouTube channel and download podcasts from iTunes. There are many additional resources I would highly recommend, too, including the ones listed here.

Recommended Websites

Kevin Davis, author of *Slow Down, Sell Faster: Understanding Your Customer's Buying Process and Maximize Your Sales* (www.toplineleadership.com).

Jonathan Farrington, CEO of Top Sales Associates, a firm based in London and Paris (www.jonathanfarrington .com).

Ron Karr, author of *Lead, Sell, or Get Out of the Way: The 7 Traits of Great Sellers* (www.ronkarr.com).

Jill Konrath, author of *Selling to Big Companies* and *Snap Selling* (www.sellingtobigcompanies.blogs.com).

Mark Sanborn, author of *The Fred Factor* (www.mark
sanborn.com).

Art Sobczak, author of *Smart Calling: Eliminate the Fear,
Failure, and Rejection from Cold Calling* (www.businessby
phone.com).

Brian Tracy, author of numerous self-improvement
books and training materials (www.briantracy.com).

High-Profit Selling is about showing you ways you can increase
the level of profit you earn from each and every sale. The top
performers—those salespeople who are at the top of the list
each and every year—are able to do it because they can cope
with any situation that crops up. They can handle shifts in
customers, weather changes in territories, and whatever else
is thrown their way, because they refuse to take a reactive
approach. Instead, they consistently take an active approach
to their job. Top performers execute the details of their job
well because they know strategically where they are going.

Before you put down this book, take the time to determine exactly what it is you are going to do differently as a
result of reading this book. If you don't do something differently, call me and I will give you your money back, because I
look at everything as having return on investment. Purchasing
this book and taking the time to read it is just that: an investment that demands a return.

Index